ESSENTIAL ACCOUNTING FOR MANAGERS

A. P. ROBSON
B.Sc. (ECON.), F.C.A., F.C.M.A.

*Former Professor of Management Accounting,
Cranfield School of Management*

CONTINUUM
London and New York

Continuum
The Tower Building, 11 York Road, London SE1 7NX
370 Lexington Avenue, New York, NY10017-6503

First published 1966
Second edition 1967
Third edition 1970
Fourth edition 1979
Reprinted 1980, 1982, 1983, 1984, 1985, 1986
Fifth edition 1988
Reprinted 1989, 1991, 1992, 1993, 1994
Sixth edition 1997
Reprinted 2000

British Library Cataloguing-in-Publication Data

Robson, A. P. (Alan Peel)
    Essential accounting for managers.—6th ed.
    1. Accounting—For management
    I. Title
    657′.024658

ISBN 0–8264–5471–2

Typeset by Scribe Design, Gillingham, Kent
Printed and bound in Great Britain by Biddles Ltd
www.biddles.co.uk

PREFACE TO THE FIRST EDITION

Essential Accounting for Managers has been written for the non-accountant manager. It is the outcome of several years' experience at Ashbridge Management College, company training centres and at the B.I.M. Oxford Course in Management Practice. The book has been written in the belief that every manager needs to equip himself with a basic knowledge of accounting; particularly in order to make informed decisions, and to see the effect of his actions, or intended actions, on the financial position and profitability of his company. Only those aspects of accounting which are considered relevant for this purpose have been included, so that the book aims to improve managerial reading on financial topics.

Accounting is seen as a useful aid to mangement at successive stages, from the analysis of a business situation, through the planning of operations and projects, to a comparison of performance with plan, the whole being carried out in an environment of change. Explanations of how figures are calculated are given at intervals throughout the book, in sufficient detail to enable the manager to understand, and make proper use of, the techniques under discussion. A chapter on more general aspects of accounting measurement is also provided. Throughout the book, detailed calculations of little value to the user of accounting have been avoided.

In this way it is intended that the book will provide a basic understanding of those essential aspects of accounting which will be of value to a wide variety of managers in their contact with accountants and accounting reports in practice. The book will also be of interest to management teachers and training officers, who are responsible for the accounting aspects of management courses, or who are running intensive appreciation courses in accounting for non-financial managers.

I would like to thank Alan Johnson, B.A., A.C.W.A., of Ashbridge Management College, and Antony Hichens, M.B.A., B.A., Barrister of Law, of the Rio Tinto-Zinc Corporation, both of whom read a section of the typescript and made a number of helpful comments and suggestions. I would also like to thank Miss Joan Elliott for the unfailing speed and accuracy with which she typed the initial drafts and the final text.

Whitchurch-on-Thames, 1966   A. P. ROBSON

PREFACE TO THE SIXTH EDITION

Since this book was first published, thirty years ago, there have been substantial changes in accounting practice, in the development of managers, and in my own approach to the teaching of the subject. I have taken account of all of these in this revised edition.

In updating my book for this edition, I have maintained the approach and style of the original: to isolate the essential elements of the subject as they relate to managers, and to explain these essentials in such a way that non-financially trained managers will fully understand, while qualified accountants will acknowledge the technical accuracy and thoroughness of what is said. I hope that this edition will be as well received as previous editions have been.

This edition provides me with an opportunity to publicly thank my secretary Marjorie Dawe, for her expert help over many years.

Cranfield, 1996   A. P. ROBSON

CONTENTS

TO
JOYCE and ANDREW

1 ACCOUNTING AND BUSINESS REALITY

Accountants do their best to translate business reality into a set of financial statements. Why do they do this ? Because various people, notably directors and managers, want to know what is happening to businesses, and they find it convenient to study financial statements in their offices as a way of finding out what is going on.

If accounting includes a process of translating business reality into a set of financial statements, what are the aspects of business reality which accountants seek to portray?

The Profit and Loss Account

When a business operates, resources are used up to produce products or services, which are sold to customers.

Figure 1 illustrates the fact that a particular business uses up four sets of resources: people's skills, services, materials and facilities, to create products or services which are sold to customers.

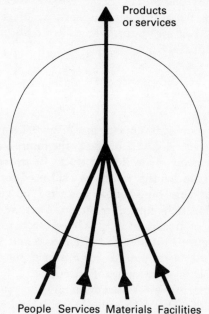

Figure 1

Figure 2 shows the accountant's translation of this activity in the form of a profit and loss account.

Profit and Loss Account for a period	£	*What is measured*
Sales	x	Value of products or services sold to customers
Costs	x	Cost of resources used up
Profit or loss	x	Wealth created or lost by business activity during the period

Figure 2

The value of the products or services sold to customers is shown as the sales figure; and the cost of the resources used up is shown as the costs figure. For a successful business, wealth is created, which in accounting terms means that sales exceed costs, i.e. the business is operating profitably.

The Balance Sheet

As a representation of business reality, Figure 1 is incomplete.

Businesses need resources for use in the future – for example, a manufacturing company will need stocks of materials for future processing; a road haulage company will need lorries for future transportation. This omission is corrected in Figure 3 where resources for use in the future are shown. They are represented by unused stocks of materials and facilities capable of further use. Notice that Figure 3 distinguishes between resources used up and resources for use in the future. For example, the diagram could represent the fact that 100 tonnes of materials have been bought and put into store and 50 tonnes used up, with the remaining 50 tonnes kept for use in the future. Also, the diagram could be showing that a lorry was bought with a three-year life of which one year has been used up and two years of the life are left for use in the future.

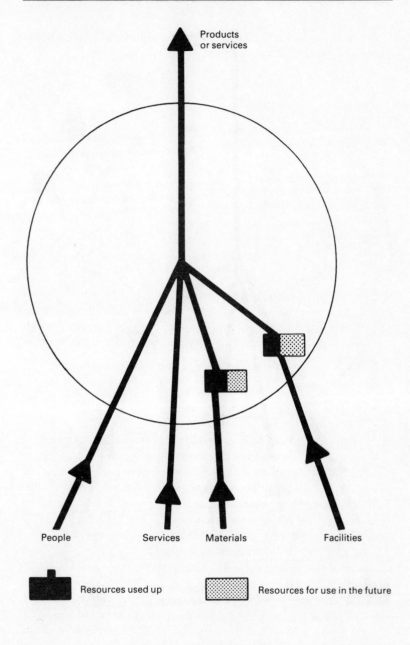

Figure 3

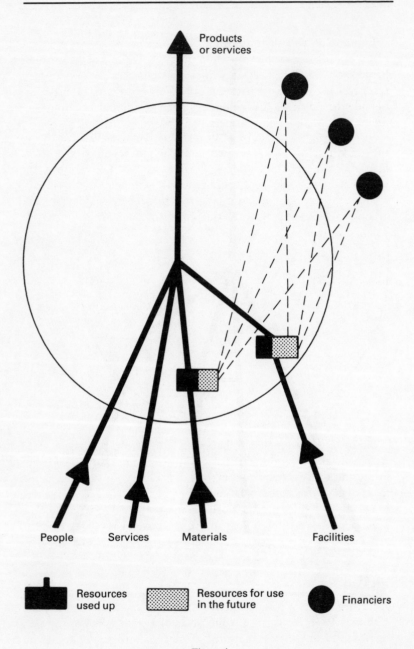

Figure 4

Figure 3 is still incomplete. It does not acknowledge that the resources for use in the future can only be obtained if the business has also obtained the necessary finance. A business can only possess resources for use in the future if groups of people, or institutions, outside the business, are willing to make an equivalent amount of finance available to the business.

In Figure 4 three groups of financiers are represented (shown as the dark circles). In a limited company these three groups of financiers are the shareholders, the lenders and the creditors, the latter being people and organizations willing to supply the resources required and not ask for immediate payment. The accounting representation of this aspect of business reality is the balance sheet.

Balance Sheet at a date   *What is measured*

£

Assets   x   Wealth invested in resources
                                                 for use in the future

£

                                                 How much finance has come
Sources of finance   x   from each source

Figure 5

Figure 5 shows what a balance sheet is. In essence, it is a statement of the wealth that has been invested in resources for use in the future, shown as 'assets'; and how much finance has come from each source, shown as 'sources of finance'. The balance sheet is a statement showing the position at a particular *point in time*, as opposed to the profit and loss account, which relates to a particular *period of time*.

The Cash Account

A further aspect of business activity is that cash changes hands. The cash may be in the form of coins and notes, e.g. sales receipts in a retail store, but in the majority of cases it will be by means of banking instruments, e.g. cheques.

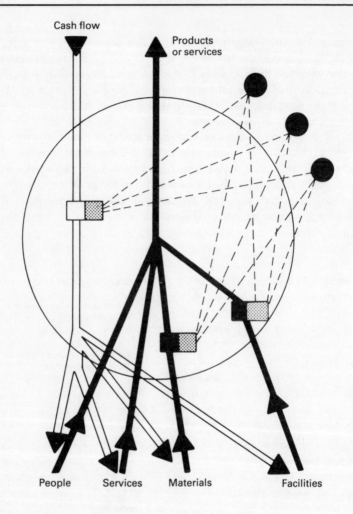

Figure 6

Figure 6 shows the cash flow from customers and to the providers of resources. These are represented by the unshaded lines on the diagram. (Other cash flows will take place, e.g. through borrowing money, but these are left out of the diagram in the interest of simplicity.) The diagram also shows that the business carries surplus cash as a resource for use in the future.

In most businesses it is very rare for the cash flowing into the business to be exactly equal to the value of the products or services sold to customers, during a particular period of time. Also it is very rare for the cash flowing out to be equal to the cost of the resources used up during the period. The fact that these two aspects of business are out of phase is partly due to the system of giving and taking credit under which most businesses operate. For example, customers may pay in advance of receiving the products or services, as is the case with people who go to the theatre or a concert, where the tickets may be bought several weeks before the performance. In most cases, however, customers pay in arrears, being given so many weeks' credit before they are expected to pay. The same is true of costs. Insurance services, for example, are usually paid for before the business enjoys the insurance company's protection; on the other hand, oil, electricity, gas and other fuels are usually paid for after they have been used by the business.

It is therefore important to monitor the amount of cash flowing into and out of the business, in addition to the other aspects of business reality dealt with so far. In accounting terms, a cash account is needed.

Cash Account for a Period		What is measured
	£	
Receipts	x	Money coming in
Payments	x	Money going out
Cash at bank	x	Money left over
or overdraft	x	or temporarily borrowed

Figure 7

Figure 7 shows the essential features of a cash account: a record of the cash receipts and cash payments during a particular period of time, together with the amount of cash at the bank. Of course, a particular business may not have any cash at the bank, in which case it is running an overdraft.

The Profit and Loss Account in More Detail

We started with the profit and loss account and saw how it is basically a statement of sales and costs. We can now expand this notion and take a look at some of the additional detail which a profit and loss account can provide for managers. There is no such thing as a standardized profit and loss account for managers in all types of business. The content will entirely depend upon what is felt to be both useful to the reader and economical to produce. We should also note that profit and loss accounts prepared for external publication and for taxation authorities will often differ from management accounts, since the basis for the first two purposes is (substantially) compliance with the appropriate legal requirements.

Figure 8 shows a basic form of profit and loss account. The cost of the goods sold is deducted from the sales value of the goods sold to produce the gross profit. The gross profit is reduced by the cost

PROFIT AND LOSS ACCOUNT
for a period

	£'000	£'000
Sales		x
− Cost of goods sold		x
Gross profit		x
− Operating Expenses		
Marketing	x	
Administration	x	
Etc.	x	x
Net profit before tax		x
− Tax		x
Net profit after tax		x
− Dividends		x
Retained profit for the period		x

Figure 8

of running the marketing, administration and other departments to produce the net profit before tax. The account then goes on to show how much of the net profit before tax is earmarked for taxation obligations; how much of the net profit after tax is for the shareholders by way of dividends; the remainder being retained in the business as an additional source of finance.

The Balance Sheet in More Detail

The next statement we considered was the balance sheet and Figure 9 shows an expanded version. The sources of finance are grouped under three headings: shareholders' capital, long-term liabilities, and current liabilities, the last two categories representing finance

BALANCE SHEET
at a date

Sources of Finance			*Assets*	Cost or Valuation	Accumulated Depreciation	Net Book Value
	£'000	£'000		£'000	£'000	£'000
SHAREHOLDERS' CAPITAL			FIXED ASSETS			
Issued shares		x	Land and buildings	x	x	x
Retained profits		x	Plant and equipment	x	x	x
		x	Vehicles	x	x	x
						x
LONG–TERM LIABILITIES						
Loans		x				
CURRENT LIABILITIES			CURRENT ASSETS			
Bank overdraft	x		Stock		x	
Creditors	x		Debtors		x	
Tax	x		Cash		x	x
Dividends	x	x				
		x				x

Figure 9

made available on condition that it be paid off at some time in the future. The assets are grouped under two headings: fixed assets and current assets. On both sides of the statement, examples are given of typical items.

Fixed assets are those resources which have been acquired with the intention that they will be kept and used by the business. As they wear out or become obsolete they are depreciated. Their net book value is the difference between their cost or valuation and the accumulated depreciation to date. They include items such as land and buildings, plant and equipment, and vehicles used by the business.

Current assets consist of cash and items which are to be turned into cash as part of the normal operation of the business. Cash will be used, among other things, to buy stocks; stocks will eventually be sold to customers who become the company's debtors; and the debtors are eventually converted into cash on settlement of the accounts. Some cash will be used buy more stocks and the cycle of conversion will repeat continually. Meanwhile, the fixed assets are used as a means by which this conversion may be carried out.

On the finance side, finance has been obtained from shareholders in the form of share capital and by retaining some of the profits belonging to the shareholders. In addition, long-term liabilities are shown, representing finance obtained on terms which include repayment more than twelve months after the balance sheet date. Current liabilities consist of items which have to be paid off within twelve months of the balance sheet date, including such items as bank overdraft, creditors (representing unpaid suppliers' accounts), unpaid tax, and unpaid dividends.

Alternative Balance Sheet Layouts

Several alternative layouts to the one illustrated in Figure 9 are found in practice. For example, continental European balance sheets may have the assets listed on the left-hand side and the finance on the right. American balance sheets may also adopt this layout and, in addition, list the items in inverse order so that, for example, the list of assets in Figure 9 would start with cash and end with land and buildings.

Another form of balance sheet is a vertical presentation in summary form, in which the longer-term investment and finance in a business is highlighted. Using only the main headings in Figure 9, the items would appear as in Figure 10.

	£'000	£'000
FIXED ASSETS		x
CURRENT ASSETS	x	
— CURRENT LIABILITIES	x	
WORKING CAPITAL		x
NET ASSETS		x
SHAREHOLDERS' CAPITAL		x
LONG-TERM LIABILITIES		x
CAPITAL EMPLOYED		x

Figure 10

(Footnotes to the balance sheet would provide the details as to the make-up of the individual headings.)

Notice that in this form of presentation the current liabilities are deducted from the current assets to show the working capital of the business. Working capital is the amount of the longer-term finance which is needed to support the current assets. To the extent that current assets, e.g. stock, debtors and cash cannot be financed by creditors and other current liabilities, finance will have to be obtained from shareholders or by means of long-term liabilities. The sum of the fixed assets and the working capital is generally called 'net assets', and the sum of the shareholders' capital and the long-term liabilities is generally called 'capital employed'.

Another form of balance sheet, which is commonly used by UK companies in their published accounts, is a vertical presentation which culminates in the figure of shareholders' capital. Figure 11 shows this layout, again using only the totals in Figure 9 (further details would be provided by footnotes). It is usually the case that UK published accounts contain some changes in terminology to accord with the UK Companies Act which governs these accounts. These changes of terminology are included in the balance sheet at Figure 11.

	£'000	£'000
FIXED ASSETS		x
CURRENT ASSETS	x	
– CREDITORS: AMOUNTS FALLING DUE WITHIN ONE YEAR	x	
NET CURRENT ASSETS		x
TOTAL ASSETS LESS CURRENT LIABILITIES		x
– CREDITORS: AMOUNTS FALLING DUE AFTER MORE THAN ONE YEAR		x
CAPITAL AND RESERVES		x

Note: 'Creditors: Amounts falling due   means   'Current liabilities'
          within one year'

        'Net current assets'   means   'Working capital'

        'Creditors: Amounts falling due   means   'Long-term liabilities'
          after more than one year'

        'Capital and reserves'   means   'Shareholders' capital'

Figure 11

Consolidated Accounts

Where a company owns more than 50% of the ordinary voting shares of another company the former is known as the holding (or parent) company and the latter is known as the subsidiary company. In this case a consolidated profit and loss account and a consolidated balance sheet are prepared. In essence, these consolidated accounts summarize the external sales and costs, and the assets and liabilities of the two companies taken together, excluding figures solely related to inter-company trading and investment. Where a company owns more than 50% but less than 100% of the ordinary voting shares of another company, the consolidated accounts will contain items relating to the minority shareholders in the subsidiary company: the amount of the subsidiary company's profit to which the minority shareholders are entitled each period will appear in the consolidated profit and loss account, and the amount of the subsidiary company's shareholders' capital, which the minority shareholders have so far provided, will appear in the consolidated balance sheet. Of course, groups of companies often consist of a holding company and *several* subsidiary companies.

The Cash Account in More Detail

Finally, we considered the the cash account. Figure 12 illustrates an expanded version.

CASH ACCOUNT
for a period

	£'000
Receipts	
From Customers	x
Other sources, e.g. share issue	x
	x
Payments	
For Supplies	x
Operating expenses	x
Taxes	x
Dividends	x
Equipment	x
Other items, e.g. repayment of loans	x
	x
CASH – at bank	x
or overdraft	x

Figure 12

The cash account itemizes not only the cash coming in from customers but other sources as well, and it shows the details of the cash payments made for supplies and for operating expenses, taxes, dividends, equipment and other items. Also shown is the cash at the bank or the overdraft, as the case may be.

Outline of the Remainder of the Book

Having established that the accounting framework consists of sales, costs, assets, finance, receipts and payments (Chapter 1), we use this framework in the context of business planning and prepare a set of budget accounts as a financial expression of a managerial plan of action (Chapter 2).

Next we look at accounting as an aid in making decisions, concentrating on two main types: projects, involving a change in the set-up by acquiring, selling or replacing assets; and decisions of a more tactical nature, where the issue is how to make more profit by a different use of the existing set-up (Chapter 3).

Planning is followed by action. As the plan is implemented, there is a need to keep a record of what is happening. Managers, as users of figures, need not know how data processing is carried out in detail, but they should be aware of the basic concepts underlying the figures in the accounting records, especially where more than one figure can be produced to represent the same set of underlying facts (Chapter 4).

During the implementation of the plan, it is necessary for managers to check performance and ask the question 'how well are we doing?' This takes the form of a comparison between actual results and budgeted results, and an analysis of why differences have arisen (Chapter 5).

Finally, from time to time it is useful for managers to carry out a corporate financial appraisal. This takes the form of a check on financial performance and financial condition, an assessment of financial structure, and a consideration of changes to the financial structure (Chapter 6).

2 PLANNING FOR OPERATIONS

Advantages of Preparing Budget Accounts

The preparation of a set of budget accounts has a number of advantages. It is a way of focusing managers' attention consciously and systematically on the future, particularly on likely developments in the environment in which a business operates, and on possible developments within the business itself. Managers are required to express their intentions for the future in numerical form, and this is likely to encourage a greater degree of clear thinking and precision than might otherwise be the case.

By expressing budgets in financial terms, by converting quantities into the common denominator of money, an additional dimension is introduced. The use of money as a common unit of measurement enables the plans of the individual members of the management team to be related to each other and summarized together. The greater possibility now exists of integrating the plans of individual managers in the various departments of the business, and of reconciling, in advance, the sometimes conflicting requirements of different departments. This integration of the planned activities of the members of the management team is a significant advantage arising out of the preparation of a set of budget accounts, as a consequence of which each member of the team has an agreed role to play in the achievement of a common objective.

The use of the money measure also enables the financial implications of budget proposals to be foreseen, and provision made for the necessary cash resources to be made available as required. The financial soundness and profitability of the proposals can also be judged in advance, by the use of ratios and other comparisons.

Finally, budget accounts and their supporting schedules provide a basis for comparison with actual performance, enabling individual managers to see where performance deviates from plan and where corrective action is required. Delegation of responsibility for the achievement of the plan, and of authority for taking corrective action, are thereby facilitated.

The preparation of a set of budget accounts may be summed up as an exercise involving both managers and accountants, requiring anticipated future events to be expressed in quantitative and money terms, integrated into a company plan and assessed from a financial viewpoint.

The Budget Period

The period of time we will adopt for the purpose of illustrating a set of budget accounts will be three months, from 1st January to 31st March. This is not, of course, meant to imply that companies necessarily adopt this period of time in practice.

Many companies adopt the practice of preparing annual budgets for operations, phased at monthly or quarterly intervals, together with a longer-term budget, possibly extending over five years or more, for expenditure on fixed assets such as the erection of new buildings.

The set of budget accounts illustrated in this chapter may therefore be looked upon as the first phase of a longer look into the future.

Budget Accounts Illustrated

In the first part of this chapter we will be tracing through the steps needed to build up a balance sheet at the close of a budget period. Readers will find it helpful to prepare their own budgeted balance sheets separately as they read through the chapter, so they are recommended to write out at this stage the headings found in Figure 30, page 34 (excluding the figures, and items in brackets) and fill in the figures for themselves as they go. Guidance for the completion of the budgeted balance sheet will be found at appropriate intervals throughout the chapter. Figure 30 will provide a check on readers' figures at the end.

The examples in this chapter will be kept simple so that the essentials of budget accounts may be understood. The general framework of a set of budget accounts will be dealt with first, using as an illustration a set of figures related to a non-manufacturing organization, followed by an outline of the additional budgets which a manufacturing organization generally requires.

Opening Balance Sheet at 1st January

In our illustration we begin with an opening balance sheet at 1st January (Figure 13). This opening balance sheet will itself be an estimate of the position at 1st January rather than a statement of the actual position, simply because the preparation of budgets will begin some time before the budget period starts.

OPENING BALANCE SHEET
1st January

	£'000		Cost or Valuation	Accumulated Depreciation	Net Book Value
			£'000	£'000	£'000
SHAREHOLDERS' CAPITAL		FIXED ASSETS	315	80	235
Issued shares	400				
Retained profits	260				
	660				
CURRENT LIABILITIES		CURRENT ASSETS			
	£'000			£'000	
Creditors	260	Stock		375	
		Debtors		300	
Tax	90	Cash		100	
	350				775
	1,010				1,010

Figure 13

Budgets to be Prepared

In order to draw up a budgeted balance sheet showing the position of the company at 31st March, it will be necessary to anticipate changes which are likely to take place in the various balance sheet items during the budget period.

These changes may be summarized by referring to the balance sheet headings in Figure 13.

On the assets side, the management of the company will have to consider what changes, if any, are likely to take place in:

1. the investments in fixed assets: whether additional items are to be acquired, or items disposed of;
2. the investment in current assets: the stock holding, and whether stocks will be built up or run down during the budget period; the debtors figure, and whether the value of customers' accounts outstanding at 31st March is expected to show an increase or decrease on the opening figure; the cash figure, and what movements of cash, in and out, are likely to take place during the budget period.

On the finance side, consideration will have to be given to:

3. any changes to the share capital of the company;
4. likely changes in the figure of retained profits due to the retention in the business of profits to be earned during the budget period. This will require a careful assessment of:
    (a) the value of sales for the period;
    (b) the cost of the goods to be sold, and the operating expenses to be incurred in running the business;
    (c) the amount of the resultant profit to be appropriated for taxes and dividends; and hence the cumulative amount to be retained in the business at the end of the period's operations.
5. changes during the budget period to the figure of creditors and to the tax liability, and whether any other liabilities are to be incurred during the budget period.

The Limiting Factor

The general scheme is therefore that budgets will be required of changes to the items listed 1 to 5 above.

The next problem to consider is the factor which will limit the scale of the company's operations during the budget period (known as the limiting factor). The scale of operations may be limited by a wide variety of factors in practice, but three of importance may be identified: sales, supplies and finance.

In most cases it is the ability of the company to penetrate the market which sets the upper limit to the scale of operations during the budget period. In other cases, however, the availability of supplies, e.g. of goods for resale, can set the upper limit. In still other cases the scale of operations may be restricted to a level which can be supported by available finance.

In our illustration of a set of budget accounts the most usual case will be assumed: that the limiting factor during the budget period will be the level of sales which can be achieved. The sales budget will therefore set the level of activity to which the other budgets will be geared.

Sales Budget

Sales budget preparation is basically the responsibility of the marketing function in a company, aided by the accountant, who may be able to assist by providing such information as trend data of sales, analysed by products, product groups, sales representatives, etc. In practice, sales budget preparation will require the preparation of a number of subsidiary schedules, generally showing quantities to be sold and budgeted selling prices, analysed by managerial responsibilities and by products or product groups.

For the purposes of illustration we will assume that the sales budget for the period 1st January–31st March relates to one product as in Figure 14.

SALES BUDGET
1st January–31st March

Quantity	Selling price	Value
Items	£	£
500,000	2.00	1,000,000

Figure 14

Later in the chapter we will discuss the preparation of a budget showing the expenses of running the marketing department. It is likely, however, that preliminary estimates of selling expenses will also be prepared at this stage, since the weight of selling effort will influence the preparation of the sales figures themselves.

Stock Budget

Closely related to the sales budget is the budget for stocks of goods to be sold to customers. The opening stock at 1st January is shown in the balance sheet in Figure 13 at £375,000, representing the cost of stock on hand at that date. Assuming that the cost price of this stock was £1.50 per unit, the opening stock figure can be summarized as shown in Figure 15.

OPENING STOCK *1st January*		
Quantity	Cost price	Cost
Items	£	£
250,000	1.50	375,000

Figure 15

A budget must now be prepared showing the closing stock position at 31st March. This budget will generally be the responsibility of the stock controller, working in co-operation with the sales manager, the buyer and the accountant. The stock budget, in many cases, will be a compromise between the requirements of these various managers. The stock controller will perhaps be conscious of space limitations in the stores; the sales manager will wish to have ample supplies to meet sales figures and maintain customer satisfaction by prompt deliveries; the buyer may prefer to buy in bulk and take advantage of quantity discounts; and the accountant will be conscious of the money locked up in stocks.

One simple approach with which to begin the preparation of a stock budget would be to use stock turnover rates. The calculation could be based on a required stock turnover rate, expressed in terms of the number of weeks' sales which are to be kept in stock. Suppose that the policy initially set for the budget period is to maintain a quantity of 6½ weeks' sales in stock, i.e. one half of the coming quarter's sales are to be kept in stock. Since stock is held in anticipation of sales, in order to assess the quantity of stock at 31st March, it will be necessary to prepare a further sales budget figure for the quarter April–June.

Suppose that a sales budget for the quarter April–June shows sales of 640,000 items. If 6½ weeks' sales are to be kept in stock, the required stock holding at 31st March will be 320,000 items (640,000 ÷ 2). If the budgeted cost price of stock is fixed at £1.50 per unit, a stock budget at 31st March can now be prepared as follows:

STOCK BUDGET *31st March*		
Quantity	Cost price	Cost
Items	£	£
320,000	1.50	480,000

Figure 16

This type of calculation represents one of the simpler methods of preparing a stock budget, and, as noted above, the results may be modified as part of a reconciliation of managers' interests. More sophisticated mathematical techniques may also be used to assist in the preparation of stock budgets. (Assuming, for illustrative purposes, that the budget is agreed as in Figure 16, the cost of stock to be held on 31st March may now be entered by readers in their budgeted balance sheet.)

Purchases Budget

The figures established so far can be used to calculate the amount of purchases required, as shown in Figure 17.

	Quantity Items	Source
Required for sales, January–March	500,000	Sales budget (Figure 14)
Required for stock, 31st March	320,000	Stock budget (Figure 16)
Total required	820,000	
Less Available from stock, 1st January	250,000	Figure 15
Purchases required	570,000	

Figure 17

Valuing this figure of 570,000 items, to be purchased at a budgeted cost price of £1.50 per unit, produces a purchases budget as in Figure 18.

PURCHASES BUDGET
1st January–31st March

Quantity Items	Cost price £	Cost £
570,000	1.50	855,000

Figure 18

Profit and Loss Budget: Gross Profit

It is now possible to summarize the monetary equivalents of the activity budgeted for so far, in the form of a profit and loss budget showing the gross profit (Figure 19).

(showing Gross Profit)
1st January–31st March

	£	£	Source
Sales budget		1,000,000	Figure 14
Opening stock, 1st January	375,000		Figure 15
Purchases budget	855,000		Figure 18
Cost of goods to be available	1,230,000		
Less Stock budget, 31st March	480,000		Figure 16
Cost of goods to be sold		750,000	
Budgeted gross profit		£250,000	

Figure 19

The inner column of the profit and loss budget shows the cost of stock on hand at 1st January, to which is added the purchases to be made during the budget period, making the total cost of goods to be available. From this figure is deducted the cost of goods to be held in stock on 31st March, leaving the cost of goods to be sold during the budget period. In the outer column of the budget, the difference between the sales value of the goods to be sold and their cost is the budgeted gross profit.

Departmental Expenses Budgets

In order to arrive at a budgeted net profit, the expenses to be incurred in operating the various departments of the business will have to be budgeted for. We will assume for illustrative purposes that there are only two departments to consider:

Marketing: including advertising, selling and distribution;
Administration: including buying, stock control, personnel, accounting and general management.

Detailed schedules of expenses will be required for each of these departments, built up by the individual managers concerned, working in co-operation with the accountant. The schedules will require details of the various types of expenses to be incurred, e.g. marketing department schedules might include details of:

    salaries
    commissions
    entertainment
    car expenses
    advertising

The expenses will be scheduled according to the responsibilities of individual managers, so that the budgets can later be used for comparison with actual performance.

Where appropriate, the departmental expenses figures will be geared to the level of activity budgeted for; sales representatives' commissions, for example, will be calculated in relation to the budgeted value of sales.

Summarized departmental expenses budgets will be required for incorporation in the profit and loss budget. The assumed figures for the purpose of illustration are as shown in Figure 20.

DEPARTMENTAL EXPENSES BUDGETS
1st January–31st March
£

Marketing	50,000	(including £5,000 depreciation on fixed assets used by the department)
Administration	150,000	(including £10,000 depreciation on fixed assets used by the department)
	£200,000	

Figure 20

(The £15,000 total depreciation expense for the budget period may now be added to the accumulated depreciation figure in the opening balance sheet (Figure 13) and a new accumulated depreciation figure entered in the budgeted balance sheet.)

Profit and Loss Budget: Net Profit before Tax

The departmental expenses budgets are deducted from the

budgeted gross profit, as calculated at Figure 19, to arrive at the
budgeted net profit before tax, shown in Figure 21.

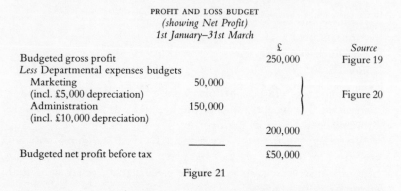

PROFIT AND LOSS BUDGET
(showing Net Profit)
1st January–31st March

		£	Source
Budgeted gross profit		250,000	Figure 19
Less Departmental expenses budgets			
Marketing	50,000		
(incl. £5,000 depreciation)			Figure 20
Administration	150,000		
(incl. £10,000 depreciation)			
		200,000	
Budgeted net profit before tax		£50,000	

Figure 21

We are now in a position to complete the profit and loss budget,
by calculating the amount of profit which will be appropriated for
taxes and dividends, and the amount which will be retained in the
business.

Profit and Loss Budget: Taxes, Dividends and Retained Profits

Taxation calculations will be performed by the company's
accountant or by the company's professional advisers, taking into
account the various tax allowances which the company can claim.
The amount of profit to be appropriated for dividends will be
considered by top management and the accountant, taking into
account such factors as the company's own needs for finance and
the rate of dividend expected by the shareholders. We will assume
that tax based on the profits for the period January–March is
estimated at £20,000, and that dividends will appropriate £10,000.

The profit and loss budget may therefore be completed as in
Figure 22.

The budgeted net profit before tax (£50,000) is reduced by the
tax (£20,000) and the dividends (£10,000) to produce the retained
profit for the period 1st January–31st March (£20,000). This is
added to the retained profits at 1st January (£260,000) to produce a
figure of retained profits at 31st March (£280,000).

In drawing up this profit and loss budget three additional figures

PROFIT AND LOSS BUDGET
(showing Taxes, Dividends and Retained Profit)
1st January–31st March

	£	*Source*
Budgeted net profit before tax	50,000	Figure 21
Less Tax	20,000	See para. above
Budgeted net profit after tax	30,000	
Less Dividends	10,000	See para. above
Retained profit for the period	20,000	
Retained profits at 1st January	260,000	Figure 13
Retained profits at 31st March	£280,000	

Figure 22

have been created which may now be entered by readers in their budgeted balance sheet.

	£'000
Retained profits	280
Tax	20
(A current liability until paid)	
Dividends	10
(A current liability until paid)	

Summary

The preparation of the foregoing set of budgets began with the opening balance sheet, followed by an assessment of the factors likely to limit the scale of the company's operations during the budget period.

The preparation of a profit and loss budget required a number of managers to submit details of their intended actions in quantities and in money terms, in the form of a sales budget, a stock budget, a purchases budget and departmental expenses budgets. In integrating these various budgets a reconciliation of the interests of the various managers concerned was required. Budgeted tax and dividend appropriation figures were also prepared, leading to a new figure of retained profits.

In this process, individual managers were directly involved in creating budgets for their own spheres of responsibility, so that

budgets have been set for later comparison with actual performance. A company profit plan has been created with individual
managers having a defined role to play in its achievement.

Further budgets must now be prepared which relate more closely
to the cash flow aspect of future operations.

Debtors Budget

Attention must be given to the changes which are likely to take
place during the budget period in the figure of debtors, shown in
the opening balance sheet at £300,000 (Figure 13). The debtors
budget will be prepared by the accountant in conjunction with
marketing management. The budget will include the opening
debtors figure, the value of invoices to be rendered to customers,
and the amount of cash estimated to be received from customers
during the budget period in settlement of their accounts.

One way of preparing a debtors budget is to establish a customer
payment pattern, for which purpose guidance may be obtained
from the accounting records.

Suppose, for example, that the payment pattern of customers is
likely to be as follows:

10% of sales invoices are likely to be paid during the month of
invoicing;

70% of sales invoices are likely to be paid during the following
month;

20% of sales invoices are likely to be paid during the next month.

These percentages may be applied to the monthly value of sales
invoices, which we will assume are as follows:

Invoices Dated	£	Source
November	150,000	From sales records or previous sales
December	300,000	budget
January	300,000	Assumed phasing of sales budget
February	300,000	January–March
March	400,000	

The budgeted cash to be received from customers may be
calculated as shown in Figure 23.

Figure 23 shows how much cash is likely to be received from

BUDGETED CASH RECEIPTS FROM CUSTOMERS
1st January–31st March

Invoices dated		Cash to be received during			
		January £	February £	March £	January–March £
November (£150,000)		30,000 (20%)	—	—	30,000
December (£300,000)		210,000 (70%)	60,000 (20%)	—	270,000
January (£300,000)		30,000 (10%)	210,000 (70%)	60,000 (20%)	300,000
February (£300,000)		—	30,000 (10%)	210,000 (70%)	240,000
March (£400,000)		—	—	40,000 (10%)	40,000
	Total	£270,000	£300,000	£310,000	£880,000

Figure 23

customers month by month, and during the whole of the budget period. Reading across the rows, it will be seen that the estimated cash receipts (£30,000) in respect of November invoices and cash receipts (£270,000) in respect of the December invoices, totalling £300,000 in all, represents the settlement of the opening debtors figure of £300,000, shown in the opening balance sheet at Figure 13.

The remaining rows in the table show the estimated cash receipts in respect of each month's invoices to be rendered to customers during the budget period. Reading down the columns we can discover the amount of cash estimated to be received in total from customers during each month, and during the quarter as a whole, i.e. £270,000 to be received in January, £300,000 in February, £310,000 in March and £880,000 during the quarter as a whole.

Using the information from Figure 23, the debtors budget can now be completed as in Figure 24.

(The debtors figure at 31st March may now be inserted by readers in their balance sheet.)

Creditors Budget

A creditors budget will also be drawn up, and in this case the accountant will probably prepare the budget in co-operation with

DEBTORS BUDGET
1st January–31st March

	£	*Source*
Debtors, 1st January	300,000	Opening balance sheet (Figure 13)
Invoices to be rendered to customers, January–March	1,000,000	Sales budget (Figure 14)
	1,300,000	
Less Budgeted cash receipts from customers January–March	880,000	Figure 23
Budgeted debtors, 31st March	£420,000	

Figure 24

the buyer. In order to calculate the cash to be paid to creditors during the budget period, percentages may again be used, reflecting the payment pattern of the company in settling its accounts with suppliers.

For illustration purposes we will assume the percentages are as follows:

0% of supplier's invoices are likely to be paid during the month of invoicing;

70% of suppliers' invoices are likely to be paid during the following month;

30% of suppliers' invoices are likely to be paid during the next month.

These percentages may be applied to the monthly value of purchases invoices, which we assume are as follows:

Invoices Dated	£	*Source*
November	200,000	From purchases records or
December	200,000	previous purchases budget
January	200,000	Assumed phasing of purchases
February	300,000	budget January–March
March	355,000	

The budgeted cash payments to suppliers can now be calculated as shown in Figure 25.

BUDGETED CASH PAYMENTS TO SUPPLIERS
1st January–31st March

Invoices dated		Cash to be paid during		
	Jan.	Feb.	Mar.	Jan.–Mar.
	£	£	£	£
Nov.	60,000	—	—	60,000
(£200,000)	(30%)			
Dec.	140,000	60,000	—	200,000
(£200,000)	(70%)	(30%)		
Jan.	—	140,000	60,000	200,000
(£200,000)	(0%)	(70%)	(30%)	
Feb.	—	—	210,000	210,000
(£300,000)		(0%)	(70%)	
Mar.	—	—	—	—
(£355,000)			(0%)	
	£200,000	£200,000	£270,000	£670,000

Figure 25

Again it will be seen, reading across the rows, that £60,000 is estimated to be paid during the quarter in settlement of outstanding November invoices, and £200,000 in respect of outstanding December invoices, making £260,000 in all, which clears the £260,000 creditors figure in the opening balance sheet (Figure 13).★ The remaining rows in the table show the cash estimated to be paid in settlement of January and February suppliers' invoices with no settlement of March invoices during the budget period. Reading

CREDITORS BUDGET
1st January–31st March

	£	Source
Creditors, 1st January	260,000	Opening balance sheet (Figure 13)
Invoices to be received from suppliers, January–March	855,000	Purchases budget (Figure 18)
	1,115,000	
Less Budgeted cash payments to suppliers, January–March	670,000	(Figure 25)
Budgeted creditors, 31st March	£445,000	

Figure 26

★ Note: Creditors are assumed to be all in respect of goods purchased.

down the columns, the table shows the estimated cash payments month by month and during the quarter as a whole.

The creditors budget can now be completed (Figure 26).

(The creditors figures at 31st March may now be inserted by readers in their budgeted balance sheet and the current liabilities at 31st March totalled.)

Cash Budget

The budgeted cash receipts from customers and the budgeted cash payments to suppliers will form part of the flow of money into and out of the company's bank account during the budget period. Starting with the opening cash position of £100,000 as shown in the opening balance sheet at Figure 13, the accountant can prepare a preliminary schedule showing the balance of cash likely to be available to make other payments during the budget period (Figure 27).

CASH BUDGET

1st January–31st March

	£	*Source*
Cash balance, 1st January	100,000	Opening balance sheet (Figure 13)
Budgeted cash receipts from customers, January–March	880,000	(Figure 23)
	980,000	
Less Budgeted cash payments to suppliers, January–March	670,000	(Figure 25)
Balance available for other payments	£310,000	

Figure 27

The balance of £310,000 will be used for such purposes as to pay taxes, to pay for departmental expenses (wages, salaries, etc.) and to make payments for any additional fixed assets which the company is planning to buy and pay for during the budget period.

We will assume that the company is planning to buy and pay for £25,000 additional fixed assets in January. (A new cumulative figure of fixed assets may now be entered by readers in the cost or valuation column of their budgeted balance sheet and the net book value of fixed assets at 31st March calculated.)

Of course such a decision to buy additional fixed assets would require careful assessment before company funds were committed. Techniques for carrying out such an assessment will be discussed in the following chapter.

The cash budget for the period may now be completed as in Figure 28.

CASH BUDGET (cont.)
1st January–31st March

	£	£	Source
Balance available for other payments		310,000	Figure 27
Less Additional fixed assets to be bought and paid for in January	25,000		See text above
Tax (see note 1)	90,000		Opening balance sheet (Figure 13)
Marketing expenses, excluding depreciation (see note 2)	45,000		Departmental expenses budget (Figure 20)
Administration expenses, excluding depreciation (see note 2)	140,000	300,000	Departmental expenses budget (Figure 20)
Budgeted Cash Balance, 31st March		£10,000	

Notes

1. For the purpose of illustration, the opening tax liability, shown in the opening balance sheet at £90,000, is assumed to be all paid in January.
2. Depreciation is excluded from the marketing and administration expenses figures in the cash budget because it does not represent an outflow of cash: it is a non-cash expense. It is assumed that all other departmental expenses relating to the budget period will in fact be paid for during the budget period.

Figure 28

The cash budget at Figures 27 and 28 shows that if the company goes ahead as planned, the cash balance will be reduced from £100,000 at 1st January to £10,000 at 31st March. (The cash balance at 31st March may now be entered by readers in their budgeted balance sheet and the current assets at 31st March totalled.)

In addition to knowing this overall change, it is also important to know how the cash figure is likely to fluctuate during the budget period. It is particularly important to know if the company is likely to go into overdraft at any time during the period January–March. If this is the case, the accountant will require to be forewarned, so that the necessary arrangements for an adequate overdraft facility may be made. A phased cash budget is therefore required, showing the balance of cash month by month. Figure 29 provides an illustration of a monthly phased cash budget, showing the sources from which the figures are taken.

The phased cash budget indicates that the company is likely to require an overdraft by the end of January to the extent of £5,000.

PHASED CASH BUDGET
1st January–31st March

	Jan. £	Feb. £	Mar. £
Opening balance—surplus (Figure 13)	100,000	—	35,000
or (deficit)	—	(5,000)	—
Receipts			
Budgeted cash receipts from customers (Figure 23)	270,000	300,000	310,000
	370,000	295,000	345,000
Payments			
Budgeted cash payments to suppliers (Figure 25)	200,000	200,000	270,000
Additional fixed assets (Figure 28)	25,000	—	—
Tax (Figure 28)	90,000	—	—
Marketing expenses (Figure 28)	15,000★	15,000★	15,000★
Administration expenses (Figure 28)	45,000★	45,000★	50,000★
	375,000	260,000	335,000
Cash—at bank	—	£35,000	£10,000
or (overdraft)	(£5,000)	—	—

★Assumed monthly phasing of cash expenses.

Figure 29

Unless the pattern of receipts and payments can be altered, e.g. by delaying payment for the fixed assets or of suppliers' accounts, it will be necessary for the accountant to arrange overdraft facilities at the bank to cover the temporary deficit. The phased cash budget emphasizes the relationship between the operational plan of management and the financing of the business. It emphasizes the point that managers, by their actions, can not only bring in cash to the business, but can create the need for cash.

For the purpose of illustration we will assume that temporary finance may be obtained from the bank and that no other loans are required during the budget period. Furthermore, no changes are planned in the company's share capital. (Readers may therefore enter in their budgeted balance sheet the same amount for issued shares as is shown in Figure 13. The budgeted balance sheet may now be totalled and agreed with Figure 30.)

Budgeted Balance Sheet, 31st March

The preceding set of budgets represents the link between the opening balance sheet at 1st January and a budgeted balance sheet at 31st March. The budgeted balance sheet at 31st March is shown at Figure 30, together with the sources from which the figures have been taken.

Summary

In addition to preparing a profit and loss budget, further budgets have been prepared which relate more closely to the cash flow aspect of future operations. These budgets were for debtors, creditors and cash. The cash budget was also prepared in a phased form. The preparation of these budgets together with the profit and loss budget enabled the accountant to build up a budgeted balance sheet at 31st March.

Additional complications found in practice have obviously been omitted from this illustration in the interest of highlighting the essential features of a set of budget accounts, and the way in which the budgets interlock. It is evident, however, even from this simple set of figures, that the preparation of a set of budget accounts involves the whole of the management team in a combined effort;

BALANCE SHEET BUDGET
31st March

			Cost or Valuation	Accumulated Depreciation	Net Book Value
	£'000		£'000	£'000	£'000
SHAREHOLDERS' CAPITAL		FIXED ASSETS	340	95	245
Issued shares (no change)	400				
Retained profits (profit and loss budget, Figure 22)	280				
	680				
CURRENT LIABILITIES		CURRENT ASSETS			
	£'000			£'000	
Creditors (creditors budget, Figure 26)	445	Stock (stock budget, Figure 16)		480	
Tax (profit and loss budget, Figure 22)	20	Debtors (debtors budget, Figure 24)		420	
Dividends (profit and loss budget, Figure 22)	10	Cash (cash budget, Figure 28)		10	
	475				910
	£1,155				£1,155

Note FIXED ASSETS	£'000	*Source*
Cost or valuation 1st January	315	Opening balance sheet (Figure 13)
Additions, January–March	25	Cash budget (Figure 28)
Cost or valuation 31st March	340	
	£'000	
Accumulated depreciation to 1st January	80	Opening balance sheet (Figure 13)
Depreciation, January–March	15	Departmental expenses budgets (Figure 20)
Accumulated depreciation to 31st March	95	

Figure 30

and that the preparation of a company plan for future operations is a comprehensive exercise linking operational plans with their financial implications.

Production and Storage Activity

If a company manufactured its own products instead of buying them ready-made from an outside source, some changes to the set of budget accounts outlined above would be required. The most important change would be the introduction of budget accounts for the company's production and storage activity.

The main features of this activity may be represented by the

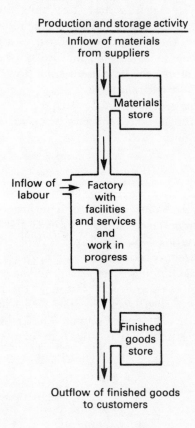

Figure 31

diagram in Figure 31, drawn up in the form of a 'bird's eye view' of the production and storage areas.

The sequence of operations represented by Figure 31 begins with an inflow of materials from suppliers. These materials flow into stock and out again to the factory, the level in the materials store rising and falling according to the balance between factory usage and replenishment.

Materials issued to the factory are worked upon by an inflow of labour, using factory facilities and services (plant and equipment, power supplies, production planning, supervision, etc.). This activity results in semi-finished work in progress in the factory, the level of which may also rise and fall.

Finished goods emerge from the factory, flow into stock and out again to customers; the level in the finished goods store rising and falling according to the balance between factory output and sales to customers. (If some items are not put into stock the flow is, of course, simpler, in that the item in question flows directly down the main limb of the diagram.)

Our task, in the remainder of this chapter, is to see in general terms how a set of budget accounts may be drawn up to reflect this activity in figure form.

Limiting Factor

An assessment will be required of the limiting factor which is likely to operate during the budget period. As in the previous illustration, three factors of importance are sales, supplies and finance. In the case of a manufacturing company, 'supplies' will include the ability of the factory to produce the required output. Factory capacity may therefore act as the limiting factor during the budget period, and this could, in turn, be due to such factors as the availability of a particular type of skilled labour, or the availability of machine capacity to produce the required output. The limiting factor will, of course, set the level of activity to which other budgets will be geared.

Factory Output

A budget will be required showing the quantity of finished goods to be produced by the factory during the budget period. For this purpose the production manager will require to establish close liaison with the marketing and stores managers and with the accountant, since the output from the factory is closely related to sales and the level of stocks.

The basic pattern of the factory output budget may been seen by working up the diagram in Figure 31. The quantity of finished goods to be sold to customers during the budget period will be adjusted for a planned build-up or run-down of stocks in the finished goods store, to equal the required output of finished goods from the factory. The calculations will therefore take the form shown in Figure 32.

	Quantity items
Required for sales	xxx
Required for closing stock	xxx
Total required	xxx
Less Available from opening stock	xxx
Factory output required	xxx

Figure 32

A close similarity will be noted between the form of this calculation and the one at Figure 17. (Instead of goods being delivered ready-made from an outside source, goods are now to be delivered ready-made from the factory.) The budgeted figures, as in the earlier illustration, will be the outcome of a number of adjustments reconciling the interests of the various managers concerned. For example, the efficiency of the factory may depend upon a steady rather than a fluctuating rate of output. On the other hand, marketing considerations may require a supply of goods which is in line with a varying customer demand. The level of stocks in the finished goods store could perhaps be regarded as a buffer between the requirements of production and the requirements of marketing management, but stores and financial considerations will also mean that the physical volume of finished goods in stock, and the consequent investment of funds, will have to be contained within limits. The preparation of a factory output

budget therefore requires a careful assessment and balancing of
these various factors, in order to reconcile the interests of the
various managers and maximize the overall company advantage.
As in the previous illustration, simpler techniques, such as stock
turnover rates, or more sophisticated techniques, such as mathematical formulae, may be used to assist in the preparation of the
figures.

Work in Progress

Where the level of work in progress is likely to build up or run
down over the budget period, the amount of factory effort required
will not be reflected solely in terms of the budgeted output of
finished goods. For example, a build-up of work in progress will
require additional effort over and above that required to meet the
output figure. Production management should therefore make an
estimate of any significant changes which are likely to take place in
the level of work in progress, due for example to planned changes
in production methods or to a planned increase in capacity
utilization.

It may be possible to express such changes in work in progress in
terms of the number of equivalent finished items which a planned
build-up or run-down represents. For example, assuming that
work in progress is considered to be, on average, half finished, a
planned build-up from 400 semi-finished items to 600 semi-finished
items in progress would be equivalent to the production of a
further 100 finished items. In this way the factory output budget
may be revised up or down, to allow for planned increases or
decreases in the level of work in progress.

Materials, Labour, Factory Facilities and Services

To refer again to Figure 31, the output figure, as adjusted for
planned changes in the level of work in progress, implies an inflow
of materials from the materials store, an inflow of labour, and the
use of factory facilities and services. Consideration will therefore be
given to the quantities and types of materials to be used, the
numbers, hours of work and grades of the workers to be
employed, and the various factory facilities and services to be used.
When translated into money terms, these matters form the subject

of three cost budgets for the factory: a materials cost budget, a labour cost budget and an overhead cost budget.

Materials Cost Budget

The preparation of a materials cost budget is greatly facilitated by the existence of standard costs. In principle, the idea of a standard cost is relatively simple; in practice the measurements required are often lengthy and complicated. Basically, a standard material cost is calculated by considering the quantity of material which should be used to produce an item of finished product, and the price to be paid for the appropriate quality of material. Standard quantity multiplied by standard price equals standard cost.

If such a standard were available, the materials cost budget could be prepared by multiplying the standard materials cost per item by the number of items to be produced (including an allowance for the equivalent items involved in a change in work in progress levels). Of course, without the existence of such a standard, the problems involved in preparing a materials cost budget would be considerably increased, and in that case, the preparation of a materials cost budget would involve considerations similar to those outlined above in connection with the preparation of the standards themselves.

A cost per item approach to the preparation of a materials cost budget may not be possible in some businesses, or necessary in others. An alternative would be to try and establish a relationship between materials cost and some other measure of activity, e.g. sales, or the sales value of output. If such a relationship were found to hold good on average, it might be possible to short-cut the preparation of a materials cost budget by simply applying the appropriate percentage to the budgeted figure of activity. Such a method might be sufficiently accurate for the purposes of budget accounts in particular cases, and, in any event, such simple average relationships are often useful as quick cross-checks on the results of more detailed calculations.

Labour Cost Budget

The preparation of a labour cost budget is also greatly facilitated by the existence of standard costs. A standard labour cost is built up by considering labour time and wage rates: the number of labour hours which should be taken to produce an item of finished product, and the rate of pay for the appropriate grade of labour. Standard hours multiplied by standard rate of pay equals standard labour cost. The calculations require a careful study of the operations to be performed in the various departments of the factory, the time to be taken and the grade of labour required.

If such a standard is available the labour cost budget may be prepared by multiplying the standard labour cost per item by the number of items to be produced (including an allowance for work in progress changes). If such a standard is not available, there is again the problem of building up a labour cost budget, requiring considerations similar to those involved in setting labour standards.

In similar fashion to the materials cost budget, the labour cost budget may also be prepared, or cross-checked, by an average percentage relationship between labour cost and an appropriate measure of activity.

Overhead Cost Budget

A production overhead cost budget represents the money equivalent of the various factory facilities and services which are to be used up in the achievement of the budgeted production activity. A summary budget will be built up from figures prepared by the various departmental managers. Where appropriate, the costs to be incurred will be calculated in relation to the level of activity budgeted for, and, in this connection, the accountant can be of assistance in analysing the behaviour of costs as the level of activity changes, so that costs which are likely to remain fixed in relation to a given variation in activity, are separated from those which are likely to vary with activity, and the rate of change of the latter established. (A further discussion of the analysis of cost behaviour will be found in Chapter 3.) Given a particular planned level of activity, such an analysis should make it easier for the managers concerned to establish budgeted cost figures for their own particular spheres of responsibility.

The overhead cost budget will cover all production costs not included in the materials and labour cost budgets, including such items as production management and supervisors' salaries, depreciation of plant and equipment, repairs and maintenance, light and heat, and power.

Having summarized these various figures, the accountant will be able to show the production cost, in terms of material, labour and overheads, of achieving the required output figure and allowing for planned changes in the level of work in progress. Similarly, he will be able to evaluate the number of semi-finished and finished items to be on hand at the end of the budget period, so creating a budgeted cost of closing work in progress and a budgeted cost of closing stock of finished goods.

Materials Purchases

The factors affecting the amount of materials to be purchased during the budget period can be seen by working up the final part of the diagram in Figure 31. The amount of materials to be purchased from suppliers will be based on the requirements of the factory for a flow of materials into production, and on planned changes in the amount of materials to be held in the materials store. The calculation of the required amount of materials to be purchased will, therefore, also be very similar to Figure 17 and is shown in Figure 33.

	Quantity units
Required for issue to factory	xxx
Required for closing stock	xxx
Total required	xxx
Less Available from opening stock	xxx
Purchases required	xxx

Figure 33

Again, the preparation of these figures will require a reconciliation of the interests of the various managers concerned – the production manager, the stores manager, the buyer and the accountant – in order to maximize the overall company advantage.

The quantity of materials to be purchased, and the quantity to be held in stock at the end of the budget period, will be evaluated by the accountant, by reference to cost prices of materials, to produce the materials purchases budget and the budgeted cost of closing stock of materials.

The Set of Production and Stock Budget Accounts

A set of production and stock budget accounts may now be prepared from the foregoing. Although having a somewhat complicated appearance when assembled together, it should be remembered that these budgets are simply a reflection, in money terms, of the production and storage activity outlined at Figure 31. Figure 34 not only summarizes the various budget accounts, but also shows opposite each account heading the equivalent stage reached in the production and storage activity diagram.

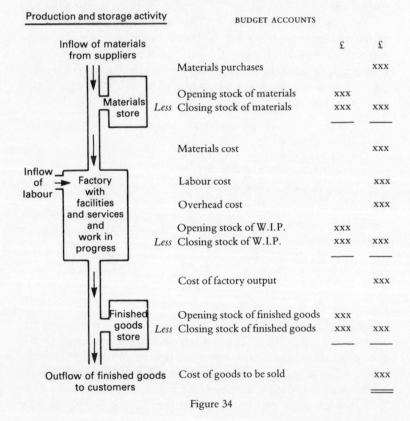

Figure 34

Conclusion

Further budget preparation will proceed in a similar fashion to the scheme outlined in the earlier part of this chapter. The cost of goods to be sold during the budget period will be deducted from the sales budget figure to produce a budgeted gross profit. Further budgets for departmental expenses, net profit, taxes, dividends, retained profits, debtors, creditors and cash will be prepared, leading to a budgeted balance sheet. The budgeted cost of closing stocks – of materials, work in progress and finished goods – will each appear under the heading of current assets in the budgeted balance sheet.

In conclusion, it should be noted that although this explanation, and the worked examples which preceded it, have traced through a sequence, it should not be assumed either that this is the only sequence which could be adopted in practice, or that the preparation of a set of budget accounts is in any way a mechanical operation. Budget preparation obviously has to follow an order, but in practice different parts will proceed in parallel, and there will be a good deal of flexibility in operation, as figures prepared previously are adjusted and readjusted in the light of subsequent calculations. Of course, individual businesses will also develop other ways of calculating particular figures to suit their own particular circumstances.

3 EVALUATING ALTERNATIVES

Two major types of decisions made by managers warrant formal financial analysis: decisions to change the set-up of a business and decisions to make a different use of the existing set-up. This chapter explains the financial techniques which help managers to make these types of decisions and provides guidance on the selection of financial figures for the evaluation of alternatives in business.

Decisions to change the set-up of a business involve the acquisition, sale or replacement of major assets, e.g. the acquisition of another factory, the sale of an unwanted subsidiary company, or the replacement of a vehicle fleet. The importance of careful evaluation of such proposals needs little emphasis because they change the basis on which future financial results depend.

Decisions to make a different use of the existing set-up involve volume and mix decisions, especially decisions to alter the product mix, the market mix or the manufacturing mix. A change in the product mix means a change in the proportion of *what* is sold to customers; a change in the market mix means a change in the proportion of *who buys* the products of the business; and a change in the manufacturing mix means a changed emphasis on *where* and *when* products are made. Price changes are often associated with mix changes.

Changes to the Set-up

The technique which is particularly relevant to the evaluation of changes to the set-up of a business is called discounted cash flow. For the purpose of explaining discounted cash flow, we will refer to a proposal to change the set-up of a business as a project.

When using the discounted cash flow technique to highlight the likely financial outcome of a project attention is focused on the amount of money the project is expected to create, or require, overall. In addition, for projects intended to earn a return on investment, it is usual to calculate the percentage return, and sometimes also the number of years needed to recover the investment in the project. These numbers are called, respectively, the project's net present value, its internal rate of return (also called discounted cash flow rate of return; discounted cash flow yield; or earning power), and its pay-back period. Two ideas which are basic to the discounted cash flow technique are cash flow and discounting.

Cash Flow in Project Evaluation

An important consequence of implementing a project is that more or less cash will change hands (the word 'cash' covers not only coins and notes, but cheques and banking instruments as well). A manager who is sponsoring a project will need to prepare a forecast of these movements of cash, showing how the project is likely to affect the bank account of the organization.

A project can affect the organization's bank account in four possible ways:

1. It can cause more cash to flow out of the bank account, e.g. additional fixed assets and stock may need to be bought, and additional operating expenses paid for.
2. It can cause less cash to flow into the bank account, e.g. existing income may be sacrificed, as when a project involves taking an existing product off the market.

The first two changes (more cash out and less cash in) make up a project's negative cash flow.

On the positive side:

3. The project can cause more cash to flow into the bank account, e.g. because of additional sales of products, or because of sales of unwanted assets.
4. The project can cause less cash to flow out of the bank account, e.g. because of savings in operating expenses and other costs, or because of additional tax allowances enabling tax payments to be reduced.

These last two changes (more cash in and less cash out) make up a project's positive cash flow.

Notice particularly the use of the words 'more' and 'less' in the definition of a project's cash flow. Only the *changes* caused by the project are being considered in order to see if these additional cash effects are wanted. This means that any cash flows that have already happened, and any cash flows which would happen anyway, should be omitted, since neither can be regarded as changes caused by the project.

Figure 35 provides a simple illustration of a project's negative and positive cash flows, laid out in a form suitable for subsequent analysis.

	Cash flow £
Now	−1,000
Year 1	+ 400
Year 2	+ 600
Year 3	+ 300

Figure 35

This shows a project with a negative cash flow initially, followed by three years of positive cash flow.

Discounting in Project Evaluation

The second idea which is basic to all modern approaches to project evaluation is discounting. Discounting is a technique which brings out the importance of the timing of cash flows resulting from a project. We can readily appreciate the importance of timing if we ask ourselves, as private individuals, would we rather have £1 now, or £1 in a year's time? We would of course prefer to have £1 now. This would be true even if there were no inflation, since we could spend the £1 immediately rather than wait for a year, or use it to pay off a loan, and so save interest during the year, or invest it at a rate of interest and receive back more than £1 at the end of the year.

Suppose, however, that we were offered the alternative of investing £1 now at 10% per annum, and recovering the £1 plus interest at the end of the year; *or* receiving £1.10 in one year's time. Ignoring tax and the possibility of inflation during the year, we would find either of these alternatives equally attractive, since £1 now invested at 10% will become £1.10 in one year's time. This equivalence may be expressed in two ways:

(a) reading forwards in the diagram at Figure 36, £1 invested now, at 10% for 1 year, becomes £1.10; or

(b) reading backwards in the diagram, £1.10 receivable 1 year hence, discounted at 10%, has a now, or present value, of £1.

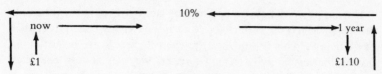

Figure 36

The second approach, which establishes the present value of a sum receivable in the future, is simply the opposite of the more familiar compound interest approach. The present-value approach is also perhaps more familiar than appears at first sight, since it is very similar to the type of calculation performed by a life assurance company when arriving at the surrender value of an endowment policy; the company establishes a present value equivalent to the sum which it would otherwise have paid out on maturity date.

The present values of future sums can be found from interest tables. Figure 37 is an extract from such a table showing the present value of £1 delayed for various numbers of years, up to 10 years hence, using four different rates of discount: 5%, 10%, 14% and 15%.

PRESENT VALUE OF £1
(Delayed 1–10 years hence)

| Year | Rate of discount | | | |
	5%	10%	14%	15%
1	.952	.909	.877	.870
2	.907	.826	.769	.756
3	.864	.751	.675	.658
4	.823	.683	.592	.572
5	.784	.621	.519	.497
6	.746	.564	.456	.432
7	.711	.513	.400	.376
8	.677	.466	.351	.327
9	.645	.424	.308	.284
10	.614	.386	.270	.247

Figure 37

In Figure 37, the present values get smaller as the waiting time lengthens, and as we have seen, this reflects the way we feel about receiving or saving cash in the future: the longer the delay, the less is the advantage to us.

But suppose we have to pay cash or sacrifice cash in the future. In this case we would prefer to pay £1 in one year's time rather than pay £1 now. This would be true even if there were no inflation, simply because, by delaying, either we can invest the cash meanwhile, if we already have it, and so earn some interest, or, if we do not have the cash, we avoid early borrowing and so save interest. Figure 37 with its present values getting smaller as the waiting time lengthens, reflects this preference for paying or sacrificing cash later rather than sooner: the longer the delay, the less is the sacrifice.

In summary, we can say that delay reduces both the advantage of positive cash flows and the disadvantage of negative cash flows, so that in the evaluation of a project, whether the future cash flows are positive or negative, they are discounted to smaller figures.

This leads us to consider the calculation of a project's net present value.

Net Present Value

We will assume for the purpose of illustration that two projects are to be considered, both requiring an initial investment of £1,000 and both yielding a positive cash flow of £1,300 over their three-year lives. The only difference between these projects is that project A brings cash back sooner than project B (an additional £100 is forecast to be received in year 1 instead of in year 2). The cash flows for each project are as shown in Figure 38.

We will also assume that both projects are required to earn at least a 10% rate of return to justify the utilization of the necessary

	PROJECT A			PROJECT B		
	Cash flow	Discount factor	Present value	Cash flow	Discount factor	Present value
	£	10%	£	£	10%	£
Now	−1,000	1.000	−1,000	−1,000	1.000	−1,000
Year 1	+ 400	0.909	+ 364	+ 300	0.909	+ 273
Year 2	+ 600	0.826	+ 496	+ 700	0.826	+ 578
Year 3	+ 300	0.751	+ 225	+ 300	0.751	+ 225
	Net present value		+ 85	Net present value		+ 76

Figure 38

finance and to allow for risk. We find from the table, under the 10% column, the present values of £1 receivable one, two and three years hence.

These present values are listed in the discount factor column of Figure 38. The cash flows are then brought back to their present value equivalents by multiplying by the appropriate discount factor. The initial investment of £1,000 for each project is not discounted because it is already at present value, i.e. it is the amount required now to initiate the project.

Project A has the higher net present value (+ £85 as compared with + £76 for project B) and this is entirely due to the timing of the cash flows in the first two years. In this case, the company concerned would rather receive an additional £100 in year 1 under project A than an additional £100 in year 2 under project B. Notice also that, even though the cash flows have been discounted at 10%, the discounted figures still show a surplus over the outlays. This indicates that both projects are estimated to earn more than the 10% rate of return used in the calculation.

The net present-value method is useful to managers in answering two types of question concerning projects:

1. Is the project likely to earn more than the rate of return used in the calculation? (The answer is yes, if the net present value of the project is greater than zero.)
2. Assuming that projects A and B are alternatives and both satisfy 1. above, which one is to be preferred on financial grounds? (Generally speaking, the project with the higher net present value is to be preferred.)

In the above calculations, 10% was assumed to be the minimum rate of return which the projects must earn to be financially justifiable. This rate must be sufficient to justify the utilization of the necessary finance and allow for risk. As we have seen in previous chapters, companies finance their operations from a variety of sources, including share capital, retained profits, and loans, so that the calculation of this minimum acceptable rate may be a complicated one in practice. It is likely, however, that the accountant will calculate a basic rate, which can be used throughout the company as a starting point in the decision as to an appropriate rate for a particular project.

Internal Rate of Return

The object of this calculation is to find the percentage rate of return which a project is likely to earn over its useful life, basing the calculation on the concept of present values. In discussing present values at Figure 38, we noted that both projects were estimated to earn more than a 10% rate of return, i.e. that a positive net present-value figure indicates an estimated rate of return on a project in excess of the rate of discount used in the calculation. Equally, a negative net present-value figure indicates a rate of return lower than that used in the calculation. It follows, therefore, that a net present-value figure of zero indicates a rate of return exactly equal to the rate used in the calculation. This is the basis of an internal rate of return calculation, which finds the rate of discount which will result in a zero figure of net present value, and this is the rate of return which a project is estimated to earn over its useful life.

PROJECT A

	Cash flow £	Discount factor 10%	Present value £	Discount factor 15%	Present value £
Now	−1,000	1.000	−1,000	1.000	−1000
Year 1	+ 400	0.909	+ 364	0.870	+ 348
Year 2	+ 600	0.826	+ 496	0.756	+ 454
Year 3	+ 300	0.751	+ 225	0.658	+ 197
		Net present value	+ 85	Net present value	− 1

PROJECT B

	Cash flow £	Discount factor 10%	Present value £	Discount factor 14%	Present value £
Now	−1,000	1.000	−1,000	1.000	−1,000
Year 1	+ 300	0.909	+ 273	0.877	+ 263
Year 2	+ 700	0.826	+ 578	0.769	+ 538
Year 3	+ 300	0.751	+ 225	0.675	+ 203
		Net present value	+ 76	Net present value	+ 4

Figure 39

Using the figures from the previous illustration, and continuing to assume that the projects are estimated to have useful lives of three years, the calculations are as in Figure 39.

In the above calculations, two different rates of discount have been tried, starting with 10%, to find the one which results most nearly to a net present value of zero. If we approximate to the nearest one per cent, these rates are: 15% for project A and 14% for project B, when the net present values in both cases are about zero.

Having established a rate of return for a project in this way, it could then be used to decide whether or not the project is justifiable financially, by comparing it with whatever minimum acceptable figure is set by top management.

The rate of return we have calculated is the return on the *outstanding* investment in a project year by year. The idea of a rate of return on the outstanding investment can be illustrated as in Figure 40, by taking the case of project A, where the internal rate of return was found to be almost 15%.

PROJECT A
(Estimated 3-year life)

		£
	Outlay	1,000
Add	15% return on £1,000	150
		1,150
Less	Cash flow year 1	400
	Outstanding investment, end year 1	750
Add	15% return on £750	112
		862
Less	Cash flow year 2	600
	Outstanding investment, end year 2	262
Add	15% return on £262	38 (approx)*
		300
Less	Cash flow year 3	300
	Outstanding investment, end year 3	0

*Includes adjustment for error, due to rounding off to nearest 1%.

Figure 40

This type of calculation is also more familiar than may appear at first sight. It is very similar to the calculation performed by a building society, where the £1,000 outlay would be equivalent to a loan to a borrower, with interest added year by year on the amount of the loan still outstanding, the calculation allowing for the fact that each year's instalment has represented part repayment of the loan and part interest.

Pay-Back Period

The object of this calculation is to find out the period of time which must elapse before the investment in a project is fully recovered. The investment in a project can be regarded either as the amount invested in it initially, or the initial investment plus interest on the outstanding investment year by year. A pay-back calculation based on the former produces a simple pay-back period, while the calculation based on the latter produces a discounted pay-back period.

The calculation of the simple pay-back period is illustrated for both projects A and B in Figure 41.

	PROJECT A Cash flow £	PROJECT B Cash flow £
Now	−1,000	−1,000
Year 1	+ 400	+ 300
Position after 1 year	− 600	− 700
Year 2	+ 600	+ 700
Position after 2 years	0 ←Pay back→ 0 (end of year 2)	

Figure 41

Both projects have a simple pay-back period of two years, after which the positive cash flow just equals the initial investment of £1,000.

Figure 42 shows the calculation of the discounted pay-back period for project A, using data taken from Figure 39. A 10% discount factor is being used, indicating that a 10% rate of interest is to be recovered on the outstanding investment in the project, year by year, in addition to recovery of the initial investment.

PROJECT A
Present value
(10% discount factor)

	£
Now	−1,000
year 1	+ 364
Position after 1 year	− 636
Year 2	+ 496
Position after 2 years	− 140
Year 3	+ 225
Position after 3 years	+ 85

Figure 42

Notice how the pay-back period now extends beyond two years. Assuming that the cash flow of year 3 accrues evenly through the year, the discounted pay-back period will occur just after 2½ years have elapsed ($2^{140}/_{225}$ years).

It should be noted that pay-back calculations, whether simple or discounted, say nothing about what happens to the cash flow after the pay-back period has been reached. Whether these cash flows are a lot or a little and whether they continue for a long time or a short time, the pay-back period is unaffected. Pay-back calculations, therefore, are *not* a measure of the overall profitability of a project. Their usefulness lies in helping to assess certain kinds of risk. For example, a company may be short of cash and may have limited access to additional finance: in such circumstances the company may prefer to undertake projects which pay back their outlay quickly, in order to minimize the risk of insolvency.

Some Further Points

Because project evaluation requires a look ahead, often over several years, many of the figures used in the calculations will be uncertain. In such circumstances it is useful to make a number of different assumptions concerning the project's cash flows, based on alternative scenarios, and see the effect of the different figures on the project's net present value, internal rate of return and pay-back period. For example, the effect of a change in government taxation and economic policy could be investigated, especially if a parliamentary election will occur during the life of a project. Similarly, the effect of a delay in the start up of a project could be studied; or the effect of more competitive business conditions. It is sometimes the case that projects are profitable in certain circumstances and not in others, and that what may appear to be relatively minor changes in the forecasts can have an important effect on the project's financial outcome. This is well worth knowing so that managerial judgement can be focused on key aspects of the proposal.

One particular factor that needs to be built into the forecasts is the rate of inflation during the life of the project. The word 'inflation' can refer to general price increases affecting the organization's financiers, or to the specific price increases affecting the cash flow of the project in question. These latter can be divided into price increases affecting cost items, e.g. wages, salaries, raw materials; and selling price increases. Building specific price increases into the calculations is an especially important point in correctly calculating the taxation effects of a project. Of course, it is also possible for prices to fall, especially the specific prices affecting the cash flows of the project in question.

Finally, it should be noted that project evaluation is part of a larger scheme of financial analysis, which can be summarized as follows: ex-post audit → project evaluation → overall budgeting. An ex-post audit is a systematic review of a past project, starting with a comparison between the forecasts made and the results actually achieved and continuing with an in-depth review of the process by which the project was evaluated, planned and executed. The object of an ex-post audit is to learn as much as possible from experience and so help to avoid repeated errors and reinforce past successes.

Project evaluation is followed by overall budgeting, in which the figures relating to each project are incorporated in the balance sheet budget, the profit and loss budget and the cash budget. An analysis of the balance sheet and profit and loss budgets may lead to the conclusion that, however desirable the projects may have been when looked at individually, some of them will have to be deferred or even abandoned because of their likely overall impact on the published accounts. Similarly, an analysis of the organization's cash budget may cause some projects to be deferred or abandoned, simply because they cannot all be afforded at once.

Summary

Three calculations of assistance to managers who are involved in project evaluation have been outlined: net present value (a sum of money); internal rate of return (a percentage); and pay-back period (a number of years). In making these calculations we noted the desirability, in the face of uncertainty, of basing cash-flow forecasts on various assumptions concerning the future. We also noted some of the issues raised by price changes. Finally, we saw how project evaluation is part of a larger scheme of financial analysis involving ex-post audits and overall budgeting as well.

Different Use of the Existing Set-up

The evaluation of proposals to make a different use of the existing set-up makes particular use of a technique called marginal costing. In illustrating the use of marginal costing, we will concentrate on the evaluation of product mix decisions. Product mix refers to the proportions of various products in a sales figure.

A change in the product mix can be achieved by expanding or contracting sales or by substitution. If sales are to be expanded within an existing set-up, there clearly has to be some spare capacity which can be absorbed. If substitutions are to made, there has to be either spare capacity to handle the expansionary element of the change, or flexibility in the situation, e.g. multi-purpose equipment which can be switched from making one product to making another.

Marginal costing is based on an analysis of costs into those that are unaffected by changes in the level of activity (fixed costs) and those that vary with changes in the level of activity (variable costs).

Cost Behaviour and the Level of Activity

The analysis of costs into fixed or variable in relation to changes in the level of activity can only be carried out according to the facts of particular cases. Statements that certain costs are fixed or variable should always be related to the underlying circumstances, so that a cost item is not fixed or variable as such, but because it has been found upon investigation to be so *in a particular case*. With this proviso in mind, we can nevertheless say that certain cost items tend, by their nature, to fall more frequently into one category than the other.

Fixed Costs

Factory rent, management salaries, insurance of plant and equipment, for example, are more likely to be classified as fixed than variable, because the range of activity within which such costs remain unchanged is fairly wide. If an investigation of a particular case shows that certain costs are likely to remain fixed in this way, they may be represented graphically as shown in Figure 43.

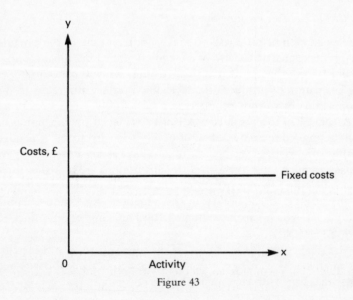

Figure 43

Costs are plotted along the y-axis and activity along the x-axis, and because the costs are considered to remain constant over the range of activity plotted, the graph line is drawn parallel to the x-axis.

Variable Costs

Certain costs such as materials are classified as variable with changes in the level of activity. Direct labour may also be classed as a variable cost, although there will be situations where labour costs exhibit a degree of fixity.

If we make the assumption that variable costs move in a straight line over the range of activity we are plotting, these costs may be represented graphically as in Figure 44, with zero cost at zero activity, and a progressive rise in cost as activity rises.

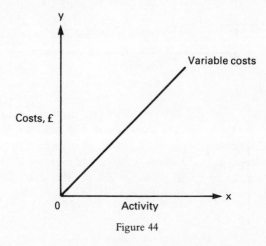

Figure 44

(The validity of the straight-line assumptions which we are making in these illustrations will be discussed later in the chapter.)

Semi-Fixed Costs

Many costs do not fall neatly into the categories of fixed or variable. They contain an element of both and are known as semi-fixed or semi-variable costs. An example of such a cost (which we will call semi-fixed) is the cost of telephones. Telephone charges are made up of a fixed cost element, the rental, which is incurred regardless of the number of calls made; and a variable cost element, the cost of calls, which will tend to vary as activity varies. Such a cost may be represented graphically as in Figure 45.

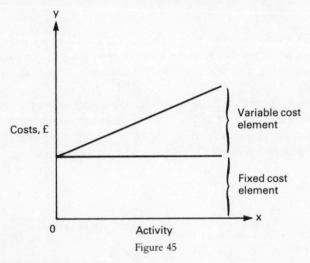

Figure 45

Repairs and maintenance to plant is another example of a semi-fixed cost. A certain amount of maintenance work will usually be necessary, even though the plant is not used (oiling, greasing, cleaning, etc.), whereas, once a plant is used, the repairs and maintenance cost will probably rise. In this case, however, it may not be possible to identify, readily, the fixed cost element in the total cost.

Scatter Charts

Statistical devices may be employed by the accountant to separate the fixed and variable elements in such a semi-fixed cost. One commonly found device is a scatter chart, on which costs are plotted against activity. Figure 46 is an illustration of a scatter chart for an assumed case of repairs and maintenance cost; each plot on the graph represents one recorded or estimated relationship between costs and activity.

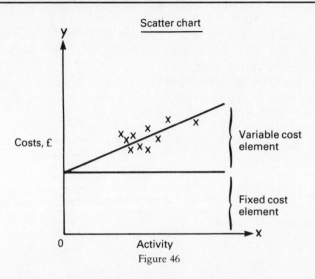

Figure 46

Having created sufficient plottings to obtain a pattern, a line of best fit is drawn through the scatter (the line may be derived by mathematical techniques or simply drawn by visual inspection). This line of best fit need not actually cut through any of the plottings, but it is drawn so as best to represent them all. The line is continued back to the y-axis, and the level of cost where it cuts the y-axis is considered to be the fixed cost element. The variable cost element at each level of activity and the fixed cost element can then be read separately from the chart. The rate of change of the variable cost element can, of course, be found by measuring the increase in variable cost following a given increase in activity.

The scatter-chart/line-of-best-fit approach is not the only way of attempting to isolate the fixed and variable cost elements in a semi-fixed cost, but other methods, in common with the one illustrated, will all produce approximate results. This approximation is a point for managers to bear in mind when using accounting reports based on a distinction between fixed and variable costs.

Profit and Loss Account Showing Contribution

Having isolated costs into fixed and variable, it is possible to prepare a profit and loss account in a revised format which will assist in making product mix decisions.

Suppose, for example, that a business sells three products A, B and C, and that the marketing manager in the business is considering a change in the product mix.

Figure 47 shows the sales and variable costs of each product and the contribution that each makes to the fixed costs and profit of the business.

	PRODUCTS			
	A	B	C	Total
	£'000	£'000	£'000	£'000
Sales	60	110	200	370
Variable costs	18	35	70	123
Contribution	42	75	130	247
Fixed costs				200
Profit				47

Figure 47

Product A is estimated to contribute £42,000, product B £75,000 and product C £130,000 towards the fixed costs and profit of the business. The total of these contributions, £247,000, is enough to cover the fixed costs, £200,000, and leave an overall profit of £47,000.

Contribution per £100 Sales

In order to establish a rank-order of the products, it is useful to know, for each product separately, the contribution to be obtained from a given increase in sales.

Figure 48 shows the contribution per £100 of sales for products A, B and C.

	PRODUCTS		
	A	B	C
	£'000	£'000	£'000
Sales	60	110	200
Contribution	42	75	130
Contribution per £100 sales	£70	£68	£65

Figure 48

Figure 48 ranks the products in order of preference: A, B, C, from the point of view of the contribution to be obtained from an additional £100 of sales income. Such a report is a useful aid in determining the priorities to be accorded to different products. Of course, the analysis is incomplete in that it leaves out of account a number of other considerations, such as the ease with which market share can be expanded, and the amount of additional promotional cost needed to change the product mix in favour of the priority products.

Contribution per Unit of Limiting Input Used

The contribution approach may also be adopted when factors other than sales limit the scale of operations of a business. For example, a shortage of labour or a shortage of raw material could each force a business to sell only what it can produce. During this period it may be considered worthwhile to change the product mix in order to concentrate on those products which yield the highest contribution per unit of whichever input is causing the limitation.

Figure 49 illustrates this approach, where it is assumed that orders exceed the capacity of a business to produce. The issue, now, is how to make the most profit from the maximum use of total capacity, assuming that the products use the same plant but require different times for the products to be produced, as shown in Figure 49.

| | PRODUCTS | | |
	A	B	C
Contribution	£42,000	£75,000	£130,000
Process hours required	500	750	1,730
Contribution per process hour	£84	£100	£75

Figure 49

Figure 49 ranks the products in order of preference, B, A, C, from the point of view of the contribution to be obtained per process hour occupied; and this ranking will be a useful guide to the marketing manager so long as the number of available process hours limits the scale of operations of the business.

Limitations and Assumptions

Managers who use marginal costing should be aware of the limitations of the data they are using. The analysis rests upon a split between fixed and variable costs and the establishment of the rate of change of the variables; but this cannot be done to a high degree of accuracy in a number of cases. Therefore the manager may be dealing with order-of-magnitude data, rather than the precise data. Furthermore, the analysis generally assumes that the variable cost per unit remains constant and that the amount of fixed costs remains constant, despite variations in activity.

It is possible for the variable cost per unit to change up or down as activity increases, e.g. overtime may need to be worked after a certain level of activity has been reached, or bulk discounts may be obtained on materials purchases, so lowering the materials cost per unit. The amount of fixed costs may also change. Fixed costs remain fixed only within a defined range of activity and this range may be more or less, depending upon the cost item in question. For example, the cost of supervision may need to be increased at fairly frequent intervals during an expansionary phase of a business, whereas the rent of the premises may remain unaffected despite substantial increases in activity. Moreover, in order to create a higher level of activity, managers may have to spend more on advertising and other promotional costs.

Contribution Pricing

The contribution approach is useful in setting selling prices in certain situations. While it is evident that managers must aim to earn sufficient revenue to cover *all* costs and earn an acceptable rate of profit, there may be situations where it is reasonable to sell individual products at a price which is in excess of variable costs only, with the result that the product makes some contribution to the fixed costs of the business.

Such a practice might be justified, for example, if a business had spare capacity which might otherwise lie idle, so that additional business could be accepted, provided it made a contribution to fixed costs. In similar fashion, an existing product might be retained, provided it made a contribution – and provided no better alternative product could be found – because by dropping the product the contribution would be lost, and some contribution to fixed costs is better than none at all.

Contribution pricing involves many considerations which are outside accounting. For example, the possibility that a contribution price will spoil the market for existing business, or that repeat orders of special business will also be negotiated on this basis; or the possibility that more profitable business may have to be forgone in the future, because capacity has been absorbed on marginal business. On the other hand, there is the possibility that a low price for a product may stimulate demand and provide a long-run profitable result, by offering the opportunity of more efficient working at higher volumes. Furthermore, a low price on one product may stimulate the sales of another, particularly if they are complimentary in use, e.g. razors and razor blades.

Nevertheless, it should be emphasized that a business survives only if it earns, in total, a sufficient contribution to cover its fixed costs and make an acceptable profit. Therefore, contribution pricing should be used with caution. It is more often appropriate to short-term situations, where the emphasis is on making the best use of available resources.

Relevant Figures

The identification of relevant figures is fundamental to the evaluation of alternatives in business. Each case will require separate consideration by the manager and the accountant jointly, to identify possible courses of action and the financial consequences of following these courses of action. Caution should be exercised in using the information contained in existing accounting reports, because information designed for one purpose is often unsuited to another purpose. Problems of alternative choice generally require the preparation of a special report, highlighting the special characteristics of the particular alternatives being investigated.

Four concepts are central to the identification of relevant figures: incremental cost, opportunity cost, avoidable cost and incremental income. Incremental cost is the cost which will be caused by the decision; opportunity cost is the financial benefit which will be lost by the decision; avoidable cost is the cost which will be saved by the decision; and incremental income is the income which will be created by the decision.

These concepts can be illustrated in a simple way by supposing that a self-employed taxi driver is trying to decide whether or not to take the afternoon off and go to the races. The cost of the decision to go to the races consists of the admission ticket and other outlays at the race course (incremental cost) plus the taxi fares lost (opportunity cost), offset by the taxi fuel not used (avoidable cost) and the hoped-for winnings (incremental income)!

These four concepts were implicit in the examples quoted earlier in this chapter. Further examples of alternatives facing managers, for which one or more of these concepts is needed are: make or buy a component or product; sell a product now or process it further and then sell it; lease or buy an asset; and a variety of proposals where the alternative is to maintain the status quo, e.g. whether or not to launch a new product, drop a product, enter a market, withdraw from a market, accept a special order, close a department, buy another business, change the pattern of working, etc.

Summary

In the second part of this chapter we have looked at some of the uses which managers can make of marginal costing, an approach which relies on the division of costs into fixed, variable and semi-fixed, and the analysis of the latter into their fixed and variable elements. Scatter charts where explained as part of this process. Marginal costing was illustrated by reference to product mix decisions, using the concept of contribution per £100 of sales and contribution per unit of limiting input used. The limitations and assumptions of marginal costing were highlighted. Contribution pricing was also discussed and its uses and dangers noted. Finally, general guidance was given on the selection of relevant figures when evaluating alternatives.

4 MEASURING PERFORMANCE

In this chapter we look at some of the more general aspects of accounting measurement which a manager should know about in order to make proper use of information which may be provided by an accountant. We will discuss important principles and conventions of accounting, but lay particular emphasis on areas in accounting measurement which require the exercise of judgement: where accounting becomes much more than an application of set rules, and where there is often no one 'right' way of measuring.

A key figure in the measurement of performance is the amount of net profit earned during a particular period of time. As we saw in Chapter 1, net profit is measured by deducting the cost of goods sold and the expenses incurred in running the business from the revenue earned during a particular period of time. Our first objective, therefore, will be to understand some of the important principles and judgements which lie behind figures of revenue, cost of goods sold and expenses.

Revenue

For most businesses, revenue is earned by making sales, and the sales figure is usually arrived at by adding together cash sales and credit sales. Cash sales are recorded at the point of receipt of the cash; but credit sales are not usually recognized at this point, but on the date of the sales invoice. The figure of credit sales will therefore be the total value of sales invoices, whether or not these invoices have been paid by customers during the period under consideration. As we saw in Chapter 1, sales invoices which remain unpaid at the end of the period (and are considered good debts) will be shown as current assets in the balance sheet, representing customers' accounts which it is anticipated will shortly be turned into cash.

For most businesses this way of calculating sales income is reasonably straightforward and is consistently applied. However, we should note that certain types of business may adopt particular ways of measuring their sales for the period. Perhaps the best known of these is in the contracting industry, where individual contracts may take several accounting periods to complete. Rather than wait until the end of a contract before recognizing that revenue has been earned, it is usually the practice to make an interim estimate of revenue earned to date, by considering *inter alia*, the degree of completion on the contract.

Cost of Goods Sold and Expenses

The net profit for the period is found by matching the cost of the goods sold and the expenses for the period, against a figure of revenue, and deducting the total of costs and expenses from the revenue. Matching implies that like should be deducted from like, so that the cost of goods sold, the expenses and the revenue should be calculated on similar bases. The accountant will therefore generally record costs and expenses as they are incurred, rather than when they are paid for.

There are sometimes considerable difficulties and judgements involved in deciding just what constitutes the cost of goods sold and the expenses for the period. In order to calculate the cost of goods sold, for example, the accountant must first decide what to include in the term 'cost'. For a trader, the obvious cost is the purchase price of the goods he buys, but it might also be argued that such costs as buying, inward freight and handling are also part of the cost of acquiring goods and making them ready for sale, and should therefore be included in the cost of goods sold figure.

For a manufacturing company, such considerations will particularly affect the way in which materials and components are costed, but the accountant of a manufacturing company is faced with a more fundamental decision as well: the problem of deciding how to

	Costs incurred £
Direct costs★	1,000
Fixed production costs	1,800
Administration department	700
Marketing department	600
Total	£4,100

Figure 50

★Production costs which vary directly with the number of units made, e.g. cost of raw materials consumed.

calculate the cost of goods made. This problem may be seen by considering the set of figures in Figure 50, for a company which has made 100 units of product during a particular period.

Full Cost

Having made 100 units of product, an immediate problem arises as to an appropriate cost for those units. One approach would be to consider that the full production costs, direct plus fixed, represent the costs of making the 100 units of product. These costs, it could be argued, are incurred in production, so that the 100 units of product which have been made should be costed at £2,800 (direct cost £1,000 + fixed production cost £1,800).

As yet, none of the units has been sold, so that included in the balance sheet at the end of the period would be 100 units of product in stock, valued at full production cost:

Stock, at cost, £2,800★

It might also be argued that the figures for the administration and marketing departments are in a particular category, in that they represent expenses of being in business and getting business, rather than part of the cost of making units of product. The following could therefore appear in the profit and loss account as expenses of the period:

Administration department	£700
Marketing department	£600
Total expenses	£1,300

There being no sales revenue, the loss for the period will be shown in the profit and loss account as £1,300.

Direct Cost

On the other hand, it could be argued that the fixed production costs should be treated in the same way as the administration and marketing department figures. The argument might be that items

★ Stock is usually valued in the balance sheet at the lower of cost or market value: hence, we are assuming that cost is lower than market value, as would normally be the case.

such as factory rent, and depreciation on factory plant and equipment are likely to continue, perhaps for a considerable time, at their present levels, despite variations in the number of units made. Therefore these items should not be treated initially as product costs, but as expenses of the period: they represent the expenses of having a factory, in the same way that the administration department figure, for example, represents the expenses of having an administration.

In this case, only the direct costs are considered to be the consequence of producing 100 units, so that these units will appear in the balance sheet at the end of the period as follows:

	£
Stock, at cost	1,000

This would mean that the expenses for the period appearing in the profit and loss account would consist of:

	£
Production department	1,800
Administration department	700
Marketing department	600
Total	£3,100

There being no sales revenue, the loss for the period under this approach would be £3,100.

It is evident that we cannot say definitely that either method is right and the other wrong, but it is also evident that the two methods can produce different profit or loss figures. This will be so whenever there is a build up or run down of stocks (in the above example there was a build up of 100 units). The two methods will also produce different stock figures for the balance sheet; direct costing always producing the lower figure.★

Cost Per Unit

One advantage of the direct-cost approach is that it eliminates fluctuations in the cost per unit of product. In the above example,

★ In the published accounts of UK companies, full costing is generally used.

100 units of product were produced at a direct cost of £1,000 or £10 each. Had the output been only 60 units, the direct costs would have fallen to £600, leaving the cost per unit the same at £10.

On the other hand, the full production cost of making 100 units was £2,800, or £28 each. Had the output been only 60 units, the fixed production costs would have remained the same at £1,800, and the full cost of making 60 units would therefore have been £2,400 (fixed production cost £1,800 + direct cost £600) or £40 each. This rise in the cost per unit from £28 to £40 is due to the fact that the fixed production costs are being spread over fewer units, so that each unit bears a larger share. Physically identical units of product may therefore be costed at different figures under full costing simply because of volume variations; whereas direct costing avoids this.

An alternative way of avoiding fluctuations in unit cost is to use a predetermined rate for charging units of product with a share of the fixed production costs: each unit of product will then be charged with the same amount of fixed production cost, even though volume of production varies. Perhaps the best known use of a predetermined rate is to be found in a standard costing system, where fixed production costs are charged at a standard rate based on a budgeted volume of production. Any variation which arises because the actual volume of production differs from the budget is highlighted as a volume variance. (A further discussion of this and other variances will be found in the following chapter.)

Changing Cost Prices

So far we have said nothing about changes in cost prices. To the extent that cost price changes occur, additional problems of accounting measurement arise, which will also affect the calculation of stock values and therefore the figures of cost of goods sold and of profit.

Suppose that items are bought (or made), put into stock and sold during a period when cost prices rise. An extract from the stock account is shown in Figure 51.

By 20th January, 150 units are in stock at a total cost of £156. The problem is to calculate the cost of the 50 units sold on 25th January and the cost of the 100 units which remain in stock on 31st January.

	IN			OUT		BALANCE IN STOCK	
	Quantity	Cost	Cost	Quantity	Cost	Quantity	Cost
	units	price	£	units	£	units	£
Jan. 1	—	—	—	—	—	0	0
Jan. 10	90	£1.00	90	—	—	90	90
Jan. 20	60	£1.10	66	—	—	150	156
Jan. 25	—	—	—	50	?	100	?
Jan. 31	—	—	—	—	—	100	?

Figure 51

First In First Out (FIFO)

One approach might be to trace the flow of costs as if they followed the normal physical flow of stock items, assuming that the oldest units are withdrawn first from stock. This first-in-first-out (FIFO) approach would lead to the following figures:

OUT		BALANCE IN STOCK	
Quantity	Cost	Quantity	Cost
units	£	units	£
50	50	100	106

Figure 52

The 50 units out are costed as if they were the first 50 units, i.e. at £1 per unit, leaving a stock of 100 units costed as 40 units at £1 each plus 60 units at £1.10 each, making the total cost of stock £106.

Last In First Out (LIFO)

An alternative approach might be based on the view that, even though the oldest units may have been drawn out first, the physical flow of goods should not govern the method of costing these units. For accounting purposes, therefore, these units could be costed on a last-in-first-out (LIFO) basis, i.e. the 50 units out could be costed as if they were the most recently acquired items. This LIFO approach would lead to the following figures:

OUT		BALANCE IN STOCK	
Quantity	Cost	Quantity	Cost
units	£	units	£
50	55	100	101

Figure 53

The 50 units out will therefore be costed at £1.10, leaving a stock of 100 units, costed as 10 units at £1.10, plus 90 units at £1, making the total cost of stock £101.*

Average Price

Another method would be to cost on a basis of a weighted average price. Figure 51 shows that 150 units have cost a total of £156, so that 50 units will have cost on average £52. Following this view, the stock account would appear as follows:

OUT		BALANCE IN STOCK	
Quantity	Cost	Quantity	Cost
units	£	units	£
50	52	100	104

Figure 54

Current Cost

The above examples have all accounted for the historical cost of the stock items in question. An alternative is to account on a current-cost basis. Under this approach the 50 units out are valued at their current cost at the date of sale, and the 100 units in stock are valued at their current cost on the stock valuation date. Suppose that the current cost is £1.20 per unit at the date of sale (25th January) and £1.25 per unit at the date of the stock valuation (31st January). The current-cost approach will then lead to the following figures:

OUT		BALANCE IN STOCK	
Quantity	Cost	Quantity	Cost
units	£	units	£
50	60	100	125

Figure 55

The 50 units out are costed at £1.20 each (the current cost at the date of sale); and the 100 units in stock are costed at £1.25 each (the current cost at the date of the stock valuation).

*In the published accounts of UK companies, LIFO is rarely used.

The examples given of FIFO, LIFO, average-price, and current cost methods have each produced different sets of numbers; nevertheless, each method may be said to represent the money measure of the same physical movement of stocks, and no one figure can be regarded as necessarily right and the others wrong. The different figures in our illustrations have simply reflected different emphases placed in the direction of current cost or historical cost levels in times of rising cost prices.

Fixed Asset or Expense

We have seen that the distinction between expenditure which results in an asset appearing in the balance sheet, and expenditure which results in an expense appearing in the profit and loss account is an important one affecting the calculation of profit, period by period. When the expenditure is considered to result in a fixed asset, particular problems of accounting measurement arise.

The first problem is to decide how much expenditure represents the original cost of the fixed asset, i.e. how much expenditure should be capitalized for balance sheet purposes. General guides would be to capitalize expenditure which is considered to benefit future accounting periods, or to capitalize expenditure which is necessary to place the asset in a working condition, in the location where it is wanted; but practice will inevitably differ in particular cases. Consider, for example, the question of delivery charges on equipment transferred from one location to another, on removal of a business from its present site. It could be argued that because these charges are part of the cost of placing the equipment in its new location, the expenditure should be capitalized. On the other hand, a more conservative course of action could be taken, to write off such expenditure to profit and loss account in the period in which the expenditure is incurred, i.e. to charge it as an expense of the period.

Similar problems arise as to whether or not installation costs should be capitalized. If such costs are capitalized, on the grounds that they are incurred in order to get the assets in working condition, further questions arise, such as whether or not part of the company's own wage and overhead cost should be included, if installation were carried out by the company's own labour force; if so, what items of overhead should be included and how much overhead would be appropriate; and whether the phrase 'installation costs' includes such items as costs incurred in removing old equipment, knocking down and rebuilding a wall, or otherwise altering a building, all of which might be necessary in order to make room for, and install, the new equipment.

Problems of definition also arise when overhauls and maintenance programmes are undertaken. The replacement of a few tiles on the roof of an office block would no doubt be considered to be a maintenance item by most people, and charged to the current period's profit and loss account as an expense; but how should we classify the complete re-roofing of a building which is in a dilapidated condition? Could it to some extent represent a backlog of repairs and maintenance inadequately carried out in the past and so charged, in part at least, as an expense, or is it to be considered an improvement and capitalized? General guides might be to capitalize expenditure which is considered to improve the asset beyond its original condition when first bought, or which is considered to extend the economic life of the asset or increase its revenue-earning capacity, but there are obvious difficulties in deciding on an appropriate figure.

Depreciation

Assuming that a certain amount of expenditure has been capitalized, so creating a fixed asset in the balance sheet, further decisions must then be made relating to:

(a)   the useful life of the asset;
(b)   the scrap or resale value of the asset at the end of its useful life;
(c)   the method by which depreciation will be calculated.

The useful life of a fixed asset is particularly influenced by three factors: the rate of physical wear and tear, the rate of obsolescence of the asset itself, and the rate of obsolescence of the product or service which the asset helps to produce. Each of these factors must be considered (not necessarily by the accountant alone) to determine which is likely to exert the dominant influence. Estimating the useful life of an asset is, of course, a difficult task, particularly for new types of assets, although for many companies, once a life has been estimated for a particular type, the tendency is to adopt standard periods of time over which similar assets are written off.

The scrap or resale value of the asset at the end of its useful life will also be considered and, if likely to be significant, will be allowed for in determining the amount to be depreciated. Finally, the method of calculating depreciation must be decided upon.

There are several methods available for calculating depreciation, three of which will be illustrated. The methods will be illustrated with reference to a fixed asset which originally costs £2,000 and has an estimated useful life of 100,000 hours over a 5-year period, with negligible scrap or resale value at the end of its useful life.

Straight-Line Method

One approach is to view the asset as equally available for use over its life, so that an equal amount of depreciation should be written off year by year. The amount to be depreciated is divided by the number of years of useful life to produce the annual depreciation charge. The result in our particular example is to charge the profit and loss account for each year of useful life with depreciation of:

$$\frac{£2,000}{5} = £400.$$

Extracts from the balance sheet, showing the cost and accumulated depreciation figures year by year, using the straight-line method, are given in Figure 56.

BALANCE SHEET (EXTRACT)

	End Yr 1	End Yr 2	End Yr 3	End Yr 4	End Yr 5
	£	£	£	£	£
Cost	2,000	2,000	2,000	2,000	2,000
Less Depreciation	400	800	1,200	1,600	2,000
Net	£1,600	£1,200	£ 800	£ 400	£ 0

Figure 56

Reducing Balance Method

Another approach might be to accelerate the rate of depreciation in the early years, on the grounds that this is the time when the asset is most efficient and so more should be charged for its services then. Progressively smaller amounts of depreciation are charged as the asset becomes less useful, because of declining efficiency and the need for more repairs and maintenance. The reducing balance method is one method which achieves this, by applying a constant percentage to the reducing net book value, period by period.

Using 40% as the constant percentage, the calculations are shown below:

	£
Cost	2,000
Less Depreciation Yr 1 (40% × £2,000)	800
	1,200
Less Depreciation Yr 2 (40% × £1,200)	480
	720
Less Depreciation Yr 3 (40% × £720)	288
	432
Less Depreciation Yr 4 (40% × £432)	173
	259
Less Depreciation Yr 5 (40% × £259, adjusted to write off the asset completely)	259

In contrast to Figure 56, the following figures would be included in the balance sheet if the reducing balance method were adopted:

BALANCE SHEET (EXTRACT)

	End Yr 1	End Yr 2	End Yr 3	End Yr 4	End Yr 5
	£	£	£	£	£
Cost	2,000	2,000	2,000	2,000	2,000
Less Depreciation	800	1,280	1,568	1,741	2,000
Net	£1,200	£ 720	£ 432	£ 259	£ 0

Figure 57

Production-Unit/Production-Hour Method

Neither the straight-line nor the reducing balance method relates the periodic charge for depreciation specifically to the rate of usage of the asset. For some fixed assets, including vehicles and certain types of plant and equipment, a fluctuating amount of depreciation based on usage may be more appropriate, so that the more the asset is used, the greater the charge for depreciation. A production-unit or production-hour method of depreciation would achieve this, by applying an estimated rate of depreciation per unit, or per hour, to the usage actually incurred.

In the above example the amount to be depreciated is £2,000 over 100,000 hours, or £0.02 per hour. This rate will be applied to the actual usage incurred during each accounting period, in order to arrive at the periodic depreciation charge.

Current-Cost Depreciation

The above calculations have all accounted for the historical cost of the asset over its useful life. An alternative is to account on a current-cost basis. Suppose that the asset is subject to price increases (for simplicity, these are assumed to occur at the beginning of each year) and that the amounts on which the calculations are based, each year, are as shown below:

for year 1	£2,000
for year 2	£2,500
for year 3	£3,000
for year 4	£3,500
for year 5	£4,000

Using the straight-line method of depreciation, and continuing to assume a 5-year life, the current-cost approach will result in a depreciation charge in the profit and loss account, for each year, of the following amounts:

Year 1	Year 2	Year 3	Year 4	Year 5
£	£	£	£	£
400	500	600	700	800
$\left(\dfrac{£2,000}{5}\right)$	$\left(\dfrac{£2,500}{5}\right)$	$\left(\dfrac{£3,000}{5}\right)$	$\left(\dfrac{£3,500}{5}\right)$	$\left(\dfrac{£4,000}{5}\right)$

Asset values, based on current cost at each year end, will reflect the fraction of the asset's life yet to be used up:

	Asset value	
	£	£
End year 1	2,000 × 4/5 =	1,600
End year 2	2,500 × 3/5 =	1,500
End year 3	3,000 × 2/5 =	1,200
End year 4	3,500 × 1/5 =	700
End year 5	4,000 × 0/5 =	0

Depreciation and Market Value

It is particularly important to note that depreciation is *not* a method by which fixed assets are reduced to their market values period by period: depreciation methods intend that market value, if any, will be reached only at the *end* of the useful life. Readers will recall from Chapter 1 that fixed assets are acquired primarily to be kept and used rather than to be sold again, so that it is not generally relevant to consider their market value period by period, unless there is a possibility of selling before the useful life has expired. Of course, the market value of a fixed asset need not equal either its historical cost or its current cost, and this is particularly true of purpose-built fixed assets which have a limited market.

Managerial and Departmental Performance

When we consider the measurement of managerial and departmental performance, it is more important than ever to emphasize that accounting should provide information which is useful to the user: in particular, that accounting information should be suited to the purpose in hand and the person receiving it.

If accounting information for managers is to yield the highest degree of usefulness, the information should, as far as possible, be tailored to the needs of the situation and the needs of the individual manager. As situations and individuals differ, there is therefore likely to be a variety of accounting information prepared for managers, and a variety of methods by which the figures are calculated.

There will also be considerable scope for the exercise of judgement in deciding just what constitutes useful information, so that the problem of selecting the most appropriate way of measuring events for managers extends beyond the selection of an appropriate accounting technique, to include an assessment of the most appropriate content of the reports presented, and the most appropriate form and frequency of presentation. Managers have a vital role to play in deciding on their information needs: they have a better knowledge than anyone else of the workings of their departments and of the issues they have to face; of the strengths and weaknesses of the system they control and of their subordinates; of the types of quantitative data which they already have available and find useful; of the kinds of things which may go wrong and need reporting on, or at least watching; of the seriousness of these adverse happenings, e.g. their repercussions elsewhere in the business; and of the earliest point at which they may be spotted.

These and similar matters are of importance in deciding on the content of reports to be prepared by the accountant; on their frequency – whether they are to be *ad hoc* reports or regular, and, if the latter, at what time interval – and on their degree of urgency. This is evidently an area of accounting measurement which managers cannot leave entirely to the accountant, if they are to receive what *for them* is the right quantity of the right type of information, at the right time. Just as managers are involved in planning for future operations and projects, with the aid of the accountant, so, too, they should be involved in the planning of their management accounting reports.

Although the ideal from the user's point of view would be a set of reports tailored to his individual needs, completely tailor-made accounting systems are rarely found in practice. This is due, in no small part, to the cost of operating such systems, and some element of standardization is usually considered desirable in the interests of keeping down the cost of accounting. The cost of the accounting system itself must be justified in terms of the benefit obtained, and a point will come in all accounting systems where the additional benefit obtained from a change is not considered to be worth the additional cost. A question such as ' Is a particular report worth producing?' will lead the manager and the accountant, jointly, to attempt a weighing up of the benefit to be obtained from a report against the cost of its preparation – a difficult exercise to undertake, since the former is an intangible and the latter usually an imprecise measurement. Nevertheless, such an exercise is essential, and should be carried out periodically, if managerial and departmental performance is to be measured economically as well as effectively.

One aspect of accounting for the performance of managers and their departments, which is particularly important, is a definition of the responsibilities of the individuals concerned and a decision regarding what constitute controllable items. Unless the figures presented to individuals relate to their own particular responsibilities and are controllable by them, little effective action can be taken following their receipt. A definition of responsibilities and a decision as to which items are controllable by particular individuals is therefore essential, and is the first stage from which individual managers can agree with the accountant on the headings under which information will be collected and reported to them. If a company operates a system of budgetary control, much of this work may already have been done, since the effective preparation of budgets by individual managers and their departments requires a definition of managerial responsibilities and a classification of accounting headings.

The financial criteria used to judge managerial performance will depend upon the financial responsibility allocated to the individual concerned. At the higher levels of management, responsibility may be for both profit and capital employed. Such a manager is often referred to as having investment centre responsibility. The financial criteria used in practice to judge his performance would be either profit less interest on capital employed or profit as a percentage of capital employed. Other senior managers may be held responsible for profit but not capital employed, in which case they are responsible for profit centres. Managers in sales and marketing may be held responsible for sales revenues and expense levels separately, in which case they may be referred to as having revenue centre responsibility. In addition, there are those (usually the majority) who are financially responsible only for the costs incurred by their departments and are therefore in charge of cost centres. Some managers are responsible for individual groups of assets, e.g. the credit controller may be responsible for debtors; the stock controller will be responsible for stocks.

Product Costs

The measurement of the cost of individual products or product groups will also involve the application of many of the principles and judgements of accounting, which have been discussed earlier in this chapter. One particular feature of the calculation of product costs, however, is the apportionment of overheads: a process which is bound to be somewhat arbitrary in practice.

Consider, for example, the case of a company which operates two production departments. Each department incurs certain costs which can be identified as relating specifically to that department, e.g. its own particular labour and material consumption costs. In addition, there will be certain costs which are incurred for the benefit of both departments, e.g. factory rent and works management salaries, which are therefore overheads from the point of view of either department. As a first stage in arriving at product costs, these overheads will be apportioned to the production departments, using bases which, for the particular circumstances of the case, are felt to give a fair share of overhead to each. Factory rent, for example, might be apportioned on the basis of square metres of space occupied, with possibly some weighting for additional amenities enjoyed in one location rather than another. Works management salaries might be apportioned on the basis of the numbers of people employed in each production department, or in proportion to their salaries and wages cost.

The creation of separate service departments, such as a maintenance department, steam and electricity generation, factory personnel department, or a factory canteen, produces further problems of apportionment, in that bases have to be found for arriving at a fair share of the service department costs to be charged to each production department. Measures of usage may be possible, such as labour-time bookings for maintenance work and meter readings for steam and electricity usage. Such measures, although possible, might not always be practicable, so that, for example, it might not be considered worthwhile installing electricity meters in every department of a large factory. In such a case, and in cases where direct measurement of services is impossible, such as with the factory personnel department, fair-share bases for apportionment have to be found.

Service departments which render services to each other create additional problems. For example, the maintenance department might serve the personnel department, which in turn serves the maintenance department. A frequently found solution to this problem is to take each service department in a particular order, and apportion its costs only once.

The process of apportionment described above enables overhead rates to be calculated so that products passing through the various production departments of the business may be charged with a fair share of overhead. Overhead rates are commonly calculated in terms of an amount of overhead per labour or machine hour, or per item of product. These rates, and the apportionment which lies behind them, are not necessarily related to a production department as a whole, but could relate to a relatively small section of a department, such as a group of machines, or even to a single machine if such a degree of detail were felt to be justified in particular cases.

A manager who is using product cost figures which are based on procedures similar to those described above, will readily appreciate that he is dealing with approximations. In order to obtain a better perspective on the likely degree of approximation in the data he is handling, it is often helpful for a manager to obtain a general understanding of the processes of apportionment carried out in his own company. Furthermore, the individual manager can often assist the accountant in deciding on suitable bases for particular circumstances.

Joint Products and By-Products

Before leaving the subject of product costing mention should be made of joint products and by-products, which arise when two or more products are made from the same raw material source, as when parts of an animal yield various meat and skin products. This situation produces considerable problems in accounting measurement, which are something more than extreme forms of apportionment problems, since *any* method of apportionment will be arbitrary.

The costs incurred up to the point of separation may be split according to a number of assumptions, but perhaps the best known methods are to split the cost in proportion to the sales value of the various products produced, or the weight of the various products produced. Joint products are thereafter costed separately as further processing continues, while the value of a by-product is usually regarded as a reduction in the total cost of the main product.

Summary

In this chapter we have been concerned with ways in which the accountant measures performance, dealing with general principles of accounting measurement, and laying special emphasis on problem areas where there is often no one 'right' way of measuring. We have discussed the calculation of revenue, cost of goods sold and expenses, together with related problems in accounting for stocks and fixed assets.

This led us to consider in more detail the measurement of the performance of individual managers and their departments, and to discuss important factors affecting the usefulness of information provided for managers by an accounting system.

Finally we considered the measurement of product cost, and discussed the various calculations which lie behind product cost figures, including the apportionment of overheads and the separation of joint and by-product costs.

5 COMPARING PERFORMANCE WITH PLAN

A comparison between performance and plan and the analysis of variances between the two is a preliminary step towards the taking of corrective action by managers: action which in most cases will be aimed at modifying future performance, but may also result in replanning, or improved planning in the future. In this chapter we will consider how the accountant can help managers in this connection, by analysing and reporting on important variances. Our attention will be focused primarily on those techniques which can help to indicate the cause of a variance and the person who is responsible for correcting it.

It should be noted at once that the interpretation of variances can only be carried out by those who are in touch with the particular circumstances of the case, and that further investigations are usually necessary, beyond figure analysis, to find out the underlying causes. It is true that, by virtue of additional information in his possession, the accountant can often add a written explanation to a figure report, so aiding the manager in his interpretation, and introducing an element of flexibility into a reporting system which might otherwise become unduly standardized; furthermore, it is always possible to design an accounting system which can enable the accountant to calculate a variety of variances by cause, so long as the extra benefit to be obtained from this information is considered to be worth the extra cost incurred. But despite this, the manager will inevitably have to fill in a good deal of background detail himself, including those factors which cannot be measured directly in figure form, such as human relations problems, which may be the basic reason why performance has deviated from plan. This is simply another example of the general point that accounting does not provide all the information (or necessarily the most important information) which a manager needs in order to make a business decision.

Nevertheless, variance analysis is an essential aid to management, because it focuses attention on the existence of a deviation from plan; on the direction of this deviation (favourable or adverse); and on its extent. Variance analysis throws valuable light on the causes of a problem, and can help to isolate those factors which are controllable by particular individuals. It can focus attention on selected areas of a business and on a limited range of pertinent information; so enabling managers to manage by exception.

Suppose that a management team has prepared the following budget:

	£	£	
Sales		7,000	(1,000 items of finished product produced, and sold at £7 each)
Labour cost	2,500		(625 hours at £4 per hour)
Materials cost	2,750		(1,250 units of material @ £2.20 per unit of material)
Variable production overhead	250		(£0.25 per item of finished product produced)
Fixed production overhead	500	6,000	
Gross profit		1,000	(£1 per item sold)
Administration and marketing		400	
Net profit		600	

Figure 58

Actual results for the period covered by the budget are:

	£	£	
Sales		6,400	(800 items of finished product produced, and sold at £8 each)
Labour cost	2,160		(480 hours @ £4.50 per hour)
Materials cost	2,800		(1,400 units of material @ £2 per unit of material)
Variable production overhead	220		
Fixed production overhead	470	5,650	
Gross profit		750	
Administration and marketing		420	
Net profit		330	

Figure 59

An explanation is therefore needed as to why actual profit is £330 when budgeted profit was £600.

In providing this explanation we will calculate variances relating to the cost items first.

Labour Variances

In Chapter 2 we saw how a standard labour cost was built up by considering labour time and rates of pay: the number of labour hours which should be taken to produce an item of finished product, and the rates of pay for the appropriate grades of labour. Standard hours multiplied by standard rates of pay equalled standard labour cost.

If we compare the actual labour cost incurred by a department in producing a certain number of items of finished product, with the equivalent standard labour cost, we can obtain a labour total variance. This variance is favourable if actual labour cost is less than standard, and adverse if it exceeds standard. Useful as it is to know that labour has, in total, cost more or less than it should, if appropriate managerial action is to be taken further analysis is needed with the aim of highlighting the underlying causes of this variance, and indicating who is responsible for taking the necessary corrective action.

Since labour cost is made up of hours multiplied by rates of pay per hour, the labour total variance may be analysed into two components: a labour efficiency variance, which arises when actual time taken differs from the standard time set, and a labour rate variance, which arises when actual rates of pay differ from the standard rates set.

In Figure 58 the standard labour cost is £2.50 per item of finished product produced (£2,500 ÷ 1,000). Therefore the standard cost making 800 items of finished product is £2,000 (800 × £2.50). This is the correct labour cost to incur in making the 800 items. A comparison between this figure and the actual labour cost of making the 800 items, £2,160 (Figure 59), produces an adverse labour total variance of £160. This is the amount of profit which has been lost by producing 800 items of finished product at excess labour cost. An analysis of this variance produces the following:

	Standard (to make 800 items of finished product)	Actual (Figure 59)	Variance
Hours	500★	480	
Rate per hour	£4	£4.50	
	£2,000	£2,160	£160 (adverse)

★If 625 hours are needed to make 1,000 items of finished product (Figure 58), then 500 hours are needed to make 800 items of finished product.

It is now possible to highlight how much of the £160 adverse labour total variance is due to the hours component and how much to the rate per hour component.

Considering the hours component first, the labour force has taken 480 hours to do what should have taken 500 hours, i.e. there has been an efficiency gain of 20 hours. At the standard rate of £4.00 per hour this represents a favourable labour efficiency variance of £80 (20 hours × £4.00 per hour).

On the other hand, the actual rate per hour (£4.50) has exceeded the standard rate (£4.00) so that the labour force has cost 50p per hour more than was intended. For the 480 hours actually worked, this represents an adverse labour rate variance of £240 (50p × 480 hours). To summarize:

	£
Labour efficiency variance (20 hours × £4.00 per hour)	80 (favourable
Labour rate variance (50p per hour × 480 hours)	240 (adverse)
Labour total variance	£160 (adverse)

Figure 60

The above variance analysis may also be represented in the form of a diagram, with hours plotted along the x-axis and rates per hour along the y-axis.

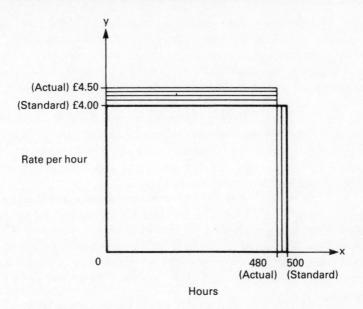

The variances can be clearly seen as the shaded areas: in the case of the efficiency variance, actual hours are less than standard, so that the favourable variance is measured by the area shaded.

(20 hours × £4.00 per hour)

In the case of the rate variance, actual exceeds standard, so that the adverse variance is measured by the area shaded.

(50p per hour × 480 hours)

Interpretation of Labour Variances

This analysis has revealed the important fact that labour cost has exceeded standard, not because of a falling-off of efficiency (there is in fact an efficiency gain), but because the standard rate of pay per hour has been exceeded. The action which should follow this analysis depends upon the particular circumstances of the case. For example, the labour efficiency variance might form the subject of praise from manager to subordinate for achieving a certain amount of work in less than standard time (a case where accounting aids the motivational aspect of management). The favourable efficiency variance might also suggest to managers that success could be repeated in other, similar, spheres of operation, so focusing attention on the performance of similar departments. Or the variance might be one of a number of favourable variances which have been consistently achieved in the past, and this may indicate that the standard itself is in need of revision.

The adverse rate variance might be a non-controllable factor, representing simply a wage award, which has occurred during the period and was not allowed for in drawing up the standard. The variance might, however, be controllable, at least in part, in the sense that local management might be empowered to offer local allowances above standard in order to attract particular grades of labour.

So far we have assumed that the labour efficiency and the labour rate variances are independent. They might, however, be interdependent, in the sense that the favourable efficiency variance could be the consequence of the adverse rate variance. Such a situation could arise where a manager or his subordinate has power to alter the composition of the labour force which is employed to achieve a given task. By employing a worker of a higher skill (and at a higher rate of pay) than that allowed for in the standard, the manager hopes to achieve an overall saving in labour cost. In our particular example, if this were the case, the action taken would have not been justified, since the higher rate of pay has not been offset by a greater gain in efficiency.

Further Analysis of the Efficiency Variance

It is often the case that the labour efficiency variance is more controllable than the labour rate variance, particularly by lower levels of management, who are usually more able to influence the time taken to do a job than the rate of pay. It may therefore be considered worthwhile keeping time records, which can reveal, in further detail, likely causes of the efficiency variance. For example, had there been an adverse efficiency variance, this could have been caused by idle time due to machine breakdown, idle time due to waiting for work, rework due to faulty material, or rework due to bad workmanship which did not pass inspection. Time records which permit further analysis under such headings can aid the manager in identifying the underlying causes of a variance; but even so, there may still be the need for further investigation, e.g. idle time due to waiting for work could be due to an understaffed production planning section, or simply due to inefficiency in the preceding section from which work is obtained.

Materials Variances

In Figure 58 the standard materials cost is £2.75 per item of finished product produced (£2,750 ÷ 1,000). Therefore the standard cost of making 800 items of finished product is £2,200 (800 × £2.75). This is the correct material cost to incur in making the 800 items. A comparison between this figure and the actual material cost of making the 800 items, £2,800 (Figure 59), produces an adverse material total variance of £600. This is the amount of profit which has been lost by producing 800 items of finished product at excess material cost.

An analysis of this variance produces the following:

	Standard (to make 800 items of finished product)	*Actual* (Figure 59)	*Variance*
Quantity (units of material)	1,000*	1,400	
Price per unit of material	£2.20	£2	
	£2,200	£2,800	£600 (adverse)

* If 1,250 units of material are needed to make 1,000 items of finished product (Figure 58), then 1,000 units of material are needed to make 800 items of finished product.

It is now possible to highlight how much of the £600 adverse material total variance is due to the quantity component and how much to the price component.

Considering the usage of materials first: actual quantity (1,400 units of material) exceeds standard quantity (1,000). This excess usage of 400 units is valued at the standard price per unit, £2.20, to produce an adverse material usage variance of £880 (400 units × £2.20 per unit).

The adverse usage variance is partly offset by a favourable price variance: actual price (£2) is less than standard (£2.20), so that a saving of 20p per unit has been achieved on 1,400 units, making a favourable material price variance of £280 (20p per unit × 1,400 units).

This is summarised in Figure 61.

	£
Material usage variance	880 (adverse)
(400 units of material × £2.20 per unit)	
Material price variance	280 (favourable)
(20p per unit × 1,400 units of material)	
Material total variance	£600 (adverse)

Figure 61

Interpretation of Materials Variances

In this example, variance analysis has highlighted a significant adverse usage variance which might otherwise have been hidden in the figures. The usage variance will generally be the responsibility of production management, whereas the price variance is more likely to be the responsibility of the buyer, so that one interpretation of the variances could be that production management should investigate the reasons for excess usage, while the buyer is to be congratulated on obtaining materials at a cheaper price than standard.

On the other hand, the adverse usage variance might be related to the favourable price variance, i.e. more units of material may have been used in production because a cheaper material was bought. The material usage variance may also be related to the labour efficiency variance: for example, inexperienced or inefficient labour may cause both labour efficiency and material usage variances to be adverse. As noted in the previous sections, further investigations will usually be necessary in order to determine basic causes and an appropriate course of action.

Overhead Expenditure Variances

In Figure 58, the production overheads have been split into those that vary with production and those that remain fixed in relation to production. The variable production overhead is budgeted at the rate of 25p per item of finished product produced (£250 ÷ 1,000) (Figure 58). Therefore 800 items of finished product should incur a variable production overhead of £200 (800 × 25p). This is the correct variable production overhead to incur in making the 800 items.

A comparison between this figure and the actual variable production overhead incurred in making the 800 items, £220 (Figure 59), produces an adverse variable overhead expenditure variance of £20. This is the amount of profit lost by producing 800 items of finished product at excess variable overhead cost (Figure 62).

	Standard (to make 800 items of finished product)	Actual (Figure 59)	Variance
	£	£	£
Variable overhead expenditure	200*	220	20 (adverse)

*800 items of finished product (Figure 59) × 25p per item (Figure 58).

Figure 62

With regard to fixed production overhead, the cost level appropriate to 800 items is the same as for 1,000 items, £500 (Figure 58), since these overheads are assumed to remain the same despite variations in production activity. A comparison between what was budgeted to be spent on fixed production overheads, £500 (Figure 58), and what was actually spent, £470 (Figure 59), produces a favourable fixed overhead expenditure variance of £30 (Figure 63).

	Budget (Figure 58)	Actual (Figure 59)	Variance
	£	£	£
Fixed overhead expenditure	500	470	30 (favourable)

Figure 63

If we also assume that administration and marketing expenses are fixed in relation to changes in the level of activity, a further comparison can be made between what was budgeted to be spent on administration and marketing, £400 (Figure 58), and what was actually spent, £420 (Figure 59), to produce an adverse administration and marketing cost variance of £20 (Figure 64).

	Budget (Figure 58)	Actual (Figure 59)	Variance
	£	£	£
Administration and marketing cost	400	420	20 (adverse)

Figure 64

Interpretation of Overhead Expenditure Variances

When interpreting overhead expenditure variances it is important to bear in mind the distinction between overheads which can be predetermined with a reasonable degree of certainty and items which are budgeted more by the exercise of managerial judgement. Many overheads fall into the latter category, including, for example, many of the costs incurred in running the training, research and development, secretarial, legal, accounting and marketing departments. In such cases it is very difficult to say with any degree of certainty how much expenditure *should* be incurred, so that judgement has to be applied in deciding what work is to be done in the department in question, and what constitutes an efficient level of operations. Where the level of cost set in the budget, although carefully arrived at, is nevertheless at the discretion of management, a comparison between performance and plan becomes less a question of assessing efficiency against an independent yardstick, and more a question of ensuring that budgets are not departed from without good reason.

Furthermore, a saving on budget may well prove to be a false economy with many of these discretionary costs. For example, a saving on inspection or on production planning in a factory may produce a favourable overhead expenditure variance, at the expense of adverse labour efficiency and material usage variances in the future. In similar fashion, a saving on training, on research and development, or on the advertising budget, may prove to be detrimental to the company's efficiency and growth prospects in the long run. This is not, of course, to imply that once budgets for discretionary costs have been set, managers should not look for economies in operation; but it does mean that with discretionary costs a favourable expenditure variance is not necessarily a good thing.

Overhead Volume Variance

So far we have been considering whether the 800 items of finished product have been made and sold at the planned level of cost. But the 800 items are themselves 200 short of budget, and so we need also to assess the effect of this volume variation.

Figure 58 shows that the business has a production facility which is capable of making 1,000 items of finished product per period. This facility has, in fact, been used to make only 800 items of finished product (Figure 59), a 20% shortfall in capacity utilization. Figure 58 also shows that the facility normally costs £500 per period to maintain, in fixed production overhead. A 20% shortfall in capacity utilization therefore means that 20% of this fixed production overhead has been wasted. This variance is called the overhead volume variance. The calculation in Figure 65 shows an adverse overhead volume variance of £100.

Budgeted production (Items of finished product) (Figure 58)	Actual production (Items of finished product) (Figure 59)	Production variance (Items of finished product)	Shortfall in capacity utilization	Budgeted fixed production overhead (Figure 58)	Overhead volume variance
				£	£
1,000	800	200 (adverse)	20%	500	100 (adverse) (20% × £500)

Figure 65

Interpretation of the Overhead Volume Variance

Differences between budgeted and actual volumes of production may arise for a number of reasons, some controllable, others not, including such reasons as machine breakdown, bottlenecks in the works, or lack of orders. Even lack of orders may be controllable in the sense that the marketing department could perhaps have been more vigorous in obtaining the required share of the market. Problems will therefore arise in the interpretation of the volume variance because of the wide variety of causes which may be operative, and the possibility that several managers may be involved, each taking part-responsibility for any possible corrective action.

Sales Variances

Assessing the effect of variances between budgeted and actual sales will also be a part of variance analysis. Figure 58 shows that the sales managers in the business budgeted to sell 1,000 items of finished product. In fact they have sold only 800 items (Figure 59), a shortfall of 200 items. Each item sold normally makes a gross profit of £1 (Figure 58). Therefore £200 of profit has been lost because of a shortfall in sales volume (200 × £1). This is called the sales volume profit variance. The calculations are shown in Figure 66.

Budgeted sales (Items of finished product) (Figure 58)	*Actual sales* (Items of finished product) (Figure 59)	*Sales variance* (Items of finished product)	*Budgeted gross profit* (Per item of finished product) (Figure 58) £	*Sales volume profit variance* £
1,000	800	200 (adverse)	1*	200 (adverse) (200 × £1)

$$\star\text{Budgeted gross profit} \over \text{Budgeted sales (items of finished product)}} \quad \frac{£1,000}{1,000} = £1$$

Figure 66

Finally, an assessment needs to be made of the effect on profit of charging higher or lower selling prices. Figure 58 shows that the sales managers in the business budgeted to charge £7 for each item of finished product sold. The actual selling price was £8 (Figure 59), an increase of £1 per item. As 800 items of finished product were sold (Figure 59), £800 (£1 × 800) has been added to profit because of this price increase. This is called the selling price variance. The calculations are shown in Figure 67.

Budgeted selling price (Figure 58)	Actual selling price (Figure 59)	Selling price increase	Actual sales (Items of finished product) (Figure 59)	Selling price variance
£	£	£		£
7	8	1	800	800 (favourable) (£1 × 800)

Figure 67

Interpretation of Sales Variances

The above analysis has shown that £200 of profit has been lost because of a shortfall in the volume of sales (Figure 66); and £800 has been added to profit because of a selling price increase (Figure 67). In many cases these two aspects will be interdependent, i.e. the selling price increase has caused the shortfall of volume. If this is the case the price policy appears to have paid off in that more has been added to profit by the price increase than has been lost by the volume shortfall. However, the degree of interdependence will vary according to circumstances, particularly the price consciousness of the customers and the availability of substitute products from competitors. There are many factors at work in the market affecting sales so that such an analysis, although valuable, is obviously again only a beginning to an understanding of the reasons why profit has varied because of sales variations.

Variance Report

It is now possible to produce a variance report, summarizing all the variances calculated so far. It is shown in Figure 68, together with the figure references from which the information was taken. In addition to the technical description of the variances, a plain English translation of their meaning is provided.

VARIANCE REPORT

		£	£	Figure
Budgeted profit			600	58
Favourable variances	*We increased our profit by:*			
Labour efficiency	Faster working	80		60
Material price	Cheaper buying	280		61
Fixed overhead expenditure	Spending less than we planned	30		63
Selling price	Charging a higher price	800		67
		———		
			1,190	
			———	
			1,790	
Adverse variances	*We reduced our profit by:*			
Labour rate	Paying too much for labour	240		60
Material usage	Using too much material	880		61
Variable overhead expenditure	Spending more than we should	20		62
Administration and marketing cost	Spending more than we planned	20		64
Overhead volume	Under-utilizing production capacity*	100		65
Sales volume profit	Not selling enough	200		66
		———		
			1,460	
Actual profit			330	59

Figure 68

* If adverse overhead volume variances are continually being reported, this could be re-phrased: we reduced our profit by 'maintaining excess production capacity'.

Further Comparisons between Performance and Plan

Provided the necessary records have been kept and the information is felt to be a useful aid to management, comparisons may be made between performance and plan extending beyond those outlined in this chapter. For example, where several materials are used, a materials mix variance may be calculated to show the effect on profit of a difference between the standard and actual mix of materials used in production. Where several products are sold, a sales mix profit variance may be calculated to show the effect on profit of a difference between the standard and actual mix of sales. A materials yield variance may also be calculated to show the effect on profit of a difference between the standard and actual yield of a given amount of material put into production.

Where variable production overhead is a function of hours worked rather than output, the accountant will calculate the variable overhead expenditure variance on an hours worked basis. In addition he will separately report the effect on variable overhead of working faster or slower than planned (a variable overhead efficiency variance).

Hours worked may also be used as the measure of capacity utilization. In this case the accountant will split the overhead volume variance into two elements: an amount caused by working longer or shorter hours than planned (an overhead volume variance, calculated on an hours basis), and an amount caused by working faster or slower than planned (a fixed overhead efficiency variance).

Finally, for businesses that use direct costing, as opposed to full costing, a contribution variance sums up the effect on profit of volume variations. This is measured in terms of the contribution to fixed costs and profit that is gained or lost by selling more or less than planned.

Some Further Points

One of the problems with variance analysis is that it can be made over-elaborate to the point that managers do not understand the meaning of the figures, as a result of which limited use is made of the information provided. It is therefore very important to be sure that the variances which are reported are useful and fully understood by the user.

Apart from the variances outlined in this chapter, comparisons between performance and plan may also be made relating to assets: for example, a comparison may be made between actual and budgeted stock levels, or between the actual and budgeted cash, debtor and creditor levels.

Comparisons may also be made in connection with individual jobs or contracts, or in connection with capital projects, to ensure that estimates of expenditure are not exceeded; and in the latter case, as noted in Chapter 3, it may also be valuable to carry out ex-post audits to see whether and why the projects have or have not yielded their expected benefits. The variety of reports which could be provided is obviously considerable, and will depend upon the circumstances of individual businesses and the information needs of individual managers.

Summary

In this chapter we have seen how the accountant can aid managers by reporting on, and analysing, important variances between performance and plan. The cost variances were divided into those relating to labour efficiency and labour rate, those relating to material usage and material price, and those relating to overheads. In connection with overheads, variable overheads were separated from fixed overheads in calculating expenditure variances. The effect on profit of production volume variations was also explained. The effect of sales variances was considered under two main headings: sales volume, and selling price. Finally, other possible comparisons between performance and plan were outlined. Throughout the chapter attention has been paid to the interpretation of the figures presented, the recognition of important interrelationships between variances, and the frequent need for further investigations before corrective action can be taken.

6 ANALYSING A BUSINESS

Four major themes need to be considered by managers when they are analysing a business from a financial viewpoint. These themes are: financial performance, financial condition, financial structure and changes to financial structure.

In exploring the meaning of these themes it will be useful to use an analogy. Suppose that you were watching an athlete running a race. You would assess his *performance* in terms of whether he was faster than the other runners, and whether he was faster than his own previous times. You would also assess his *condition* before, during and at the end of the race. In analysing why certain athletes both perform well and maintain a good condition you would note that they have a certain type of body *structure* suited to the sport they are engaged in. Moreover, anyone who does not have such a structure and wishes to excel in that particular sport would have to *change his structure*, e.g. build certain muscles, in order to achieve his ambition.

Similar issues apply in business. Managers should be concerned to see that they are creating a good *financial performance* (in comparison with the results of competitors and previous results). Financial performance should be accompanied by the continued maintenance of a sound *financial condition*. Managers should also be concerned about *financial structure* – how the business has been put together financially – because future financial performance and condition depend to some considerable extent on the financial structure that has been created. Finally, managers should also consider *changes to financial structure* and ask: does anything need to be done to change the financial structure of the business, in the light of changes in business conditions? They should also ask: what effect will our business decisions have on the financial structure?

Financial Performance

Financial performance measures, taken from accounts, centre on ratios related to profitability, especially the amount of profit earned during a period of time in relation to the capital employed in a business. Before discussing these ratios, however, it should be noted that capital employed is a term which is capable of a variety of definitions. The commonest found in practice are: capital

99

employed equals shareholders' capital; and capital employed equals shareholders' capital plus long-term liabilities, but in addition it is possible to find businesses where capital employed is defined as total assets, or in other ways.

The profit figure used depends upon the definition of capital employed. For example, if shareholders' capital is used, a figure of net profit after tax will generally be applicable. This is the amount of profit available to the shareholders after all expenses and taxes have been provided for. On the other hand, if shareholders' capital plus long-term liabilities is to be used, then the profit figure will generally be taken before deducting long-term interest and tax, representing the pre-tax reward to both sources of finance.

Whichever definitions of profit and capital employed are adopted, profitability ratios focus on three themes: return on capital employed, profit margin and capital turnover. These three are interrelated, as can be seen in Figure 69.

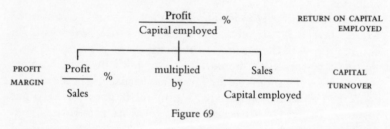

Figure 69

The return on capital employed = profit margin × capital turnover. ('Sales' cancels out when the two are multiplied together.)

It is evident from Figure 69 that an acceptable return on capital employed can be achieved by various combinations of profit margin and capital turnover. For example, certain types of retail businesses such as cut-price stores, operate on low profit margins, but carry fast moving stocks, and in some cases also carry a relatively low investment in fixed assets (such as shop fittings and delivery vehicles) in relation to their sales. These businesses operate on a low profit margin in combination with a high capital turnover to produce an acceptable return on capital employed.

On the other hand, some businesses might have a low capital turnover and a high profit margin. An example might be a spare-parts manufacturer, who may require to own relatively expensive equipment and will probably carry stocks of slow-moving parts, following a policy of being able to satisfy customer demand whenever possible. Such a business would compensate for a low capital turnover by a high profit margin, to produce an acceptable return on capital employed.

Both the profit margin and the capital turnover may be analysed further. An example of such an analysis is given in Figure 70.

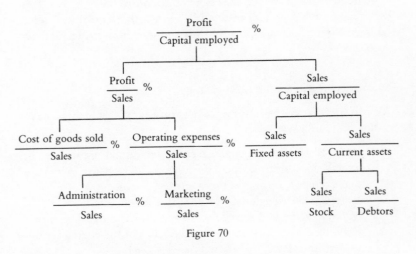

Figure 70

The profit/sales percentage will be affected by the costs and expenses incurred in earning the profit. Figure 70 illustrates three items particularly affecting the profit/sales percentage: cost of goods sold, administration expenses and marketing expenses. These items are each expressed as a percentage of sales to give an indication of the proportion of sales income absorbed by each. Further departmental or expense breakdowns could of course be provided, to suit particular businesses or particular circumstances.

On the capital turnover side of Figure 70, since capital is employed in both fixed and current assets, the sales/capital employed ratio may be broken down into sales/fixed assets and sales/current assets. Changes in the sales/fixed assets ratio could be used as an approximate indicator of capacity utilization: a measure of how hard the fixed assets are being worked. The sales/current assets ratio is perhaps more useful if broken down into its main constituents: sales/stock and sales/debtors.

The sales/stock ratio is an approximate indicator of the rate of turnover of stock: an approximate guide to the speed with which stock moves through the business.* The sales/debtors ratio is an indicator of the speed with which customers settle their accounts on average, so that, for example, if annual credit sales were £1,200, and customers' accounts outstanding were on average £200, the sales/debtors ratio would be 1,200/200, or 6 times a year. A turnover of 6 times a year would indicate that customers were taking 12/6, or 2 months' credit, on average, before they paid their accounts.

Summary of Ratios Related to Profitability

We can summarize the ratios related to profitability which we have outlined, as follows:

1. *Profit % Capital Employed.* Return on capital employed: an overall indicator of the effectiveness of the use made by management of the resources entrusted to it.
2. *Sales/Capital Employed.* Capital turnover: the amount of business generated in relation to the capital employed.
3. *Profit % Sales.* Profit margin: a measure of the average profit earned on sales.
4. 5. and 6. *Cost of Goods Sold, Administration and Marketing Expenses % Sales.* Indicators of the proportion of sales income absorbed by important items of costs and expenses.
7. *Sales/Fixed Assets.* An indicator of the value of business generated with the use of the assets which are to be kept and used.
8. *Sales/Current Assets.* An indicator of the rate of turnover of assets which are in the process of conversion into cash.
9. *Sales/Stock.* An approximate indicator of the rate of turnover of stock, providing an approximate guide to the speed with which stock moves through the business.

---

* More accurate stock turnover ratios may be calculated, e.g. cost of goods sold/stock. Another stock turnover ratio, based on quantities, was illustrated in Chapter 2.

10. *Sales/Debtors.* An indicator of debtors' turnover, measuring the speed with which customers settle their accounts on average. This ratio can also be expressed in (say) months, to give a clearer picture of the average time customers are taking to pay.

These ratios are used to assess trends, and to make comparisons with other businesses and with industry averages.

Financial Condition

Measures of the financial condition of a business, taken from accounts, centre on ratios related to liquidity and solvency. These ratios are an aid in assessing the ability of a business to pay its liabilities. Ratios related to liquidity focus on the ability of the business to pay in relation to its current liabilities, whereas ratios related to solvency focus on the ability of the business to pay in relation to its long-term liabilities.

In order to test the liquidity position of a business it is usual to calculate the ratio of current assets to current liabilities (the 'current ratio') and the ratio of cash★ plus debtors to current liabilities (the 'acid test ratio'). The acid test ratio omits the stock, which is usually furthest away from cash, to make a comparison between the total of ready money and near-ready money and the current liabilities.

It is also usual to look at the make-up of the current assets and the current liabilities, as the same ratio of current assets to current liabilities could exist even though the mixture of items within the total differed. For example, the same current assets could contain a high or low proportion of cash, while the same current liabilities could contain a high or low proportion of items not due for settlement for several months. Furthermore, it is usual to look at some of the turnover ratios described earlier. This is because liquidity ratios say nothing about time delays, e.g. how long it takes before the stock is sold, how long before the customers pay, and how long before the suppliers are paid.

★ Cash for this purpose also includes such items as short-term investments which could be turned into cash at relatively short notice.

The turnover ratios which are useful in assessing liquidity are: sales/stock, which provides an approximate guide to the speed with which stock moves through the business; and sales/debtors, which measures the speed with which customers settle their accounts on average. These two ratios give an indication of the speed with which stock and debtors are moving towards cash.

It may also be possible to measure the speed with which cash moves in the other direction, towards creditors, by calculating the average period of credit which a business is taking before paying its suppliers. This is commonly measured by the ratio purchases/creditors, so that if annual purchases were £960 and suppliers' accounts outstanding were on average £120, the purchases/creditors ratio would be 960/120 or 8 times a year. A turnover of 8 times a year would indicate that the business was taking 12/8, or 1½ months' credit, · on average, before paying its suppliers' accounts.

In order to test the solvency position of a business it is usual to calculate the ratio of long-term liabilities to capital employed. Capital employed is defined as the sum of the shareholders' capital and the long-term liabilities. Figure 10 (Chapter 1) provided a balance sheet layout which enabled this ratio to be easily calculated.

The ratio of long-term liabilities to capital employed provides an indication of the extent to which the business has incurred obligations to pay back loan capital in the longer term.

It is also usual to calculate interest cover. This is calculated from the profit and loss account and is the ratio of the profit before interest to the interest expense. For example a profit, before deducting interest, of £60, followed by an interest expense of £10 results in a ratio of 6. This means that profit could fall to 1/6th of its present amount and the interest could still be paid out of profits, once they are realized in cash.

Both the liquidity and the solvency ratios are used to assess trends, and to make comparisons with other businesses and with industry averages.

Some Dangers and Limitations of Ratio Analysis

While ratio analysis of accounts is an important tool in analysing a business, it is necessary to introduce an element of caution. Four dangers and limitations are worth highlighting:

1. A balance sheet is a snapshot picture of the state of a business at a moment in time, although in reality the picture will be continually changing. The balance sheet may not, therefore, always be representative of the average position. This is a particular possibility in businesses affected by the seasons, where the assets and liabilities can be significantly different, according to whether the balance sheet has been drawn up at the high or low season date.

2. Inflation has caused asset values to change, and these changes may or may not be reflected in the balance sheet. Because there is a possibility that assets may have been acquired or valued on different dates at different price levels, comparisons between one set of figures and another in times of inflation *might*, therefore, be misleading.

3. Accounting figures may have been calculated differently in different businesses, as there is often more than one method of calculation which can be adopted. This particularly affects the fixed assets and stock figures, and the calculation of profit, as we saw in more detail in Chapter 4. Comparisons between figures for different businesses, therefore, *might* be subject to error because of the possibility that different methods of calculation have been adopted.

4. Managers should not feel that ratio analysis will provide an easy road to the solution of business problems. Such analysis should be looked upon more as a logical way of beginning an assessment of a business situation, which should enable the manager to focus his attention on some of its essential features, and stimulate him to ask further pertinent questions. For example, ratio analysis might indicate that a trend towards lower profitability was due to a worsening sales/debtors ratio. But this in turn might be caused by bad credit control at the stage of opening new customers' accounts; failure to invoice promptly; failure to send out statements promptly; failure to review overdue accounts periodically; failure to send out reminders to customers who are late in payment; shortage of staff in the invoicing or accounting sections; or simply by a general softening of trade in which customers are taking longer to pay because they are short of cash. The sales/debtors ratio will not pin-point which of these particular factors is at work in

the situation, but it has guided the manager to a selected area of the business which appears to need attention. Only after further investigation, however, including an assessment of the human factors in the situation, will the manager be in a position to decide what action, if any, is needed.

Financial Structure

The way a business has been put together, financially, affects the profitability ratios, the liquidity and solvency ratios and cash flow. There are three major themes in an assessment of financial structure: cost structure, finance structure and working capital structure. The first two particularly affect the profitability ratios, the second particularly affects the solvency ratios and the third particularly affects the liquidity ratios and cash flow.

Cost Structure

In Chapter 3 we discussed the distinction between fixed and variable costs. Fixed costs were seen to be those costs which are unaffected by changes in the level of activity, within defined limits; while variable costs were those costs that vary with changes in the level of activity. If fixed and variable costs are plotted on a graph the cost structure of a business becomes apparent and if income is also plotted the profit or loss at various levels of activity is displayed. Figure 71 shows a business with relatively high fixed costs and relatively low variable costs.

In Figure 71 variable costs are plotted first and the fixed costs added to produce the total costs line. Activity is measured on the x-axis in units of output; values are measured on the y-axis. The sales line in Figure 71 shows the income earned by the business at various levels of activity. The point where the sales line cuts the total costs line is the break-even point for the business: the point of no profit, no loss. This occurs when activity reaches the level measured by the distance 0A.

Profits are measured in the area shaded

Losses are measured in the area shaded

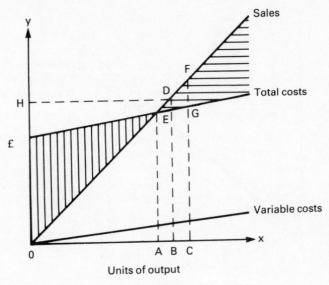

Figure 71

At the present level of activity, which we will assume is measured by the distance 0B, we can read off the profit to be earned if this level of activity continues, measured by the distance DE.

The break-even chart also shows the difference between the present level of activity and the break-even level. This difference, AB, is known as the margin of safety, and is the amount by which activity could fall back from the present level before losses are incurred.

It is also possible to obtain from the break-even chart a visual impression of the rate of change of profit. If, for example, activity is increased from 0B to 0C, profit rises from DE to FG. The amount by which profit changes, following a given change in activity, will obviously depend upon the width of the angle between the sales and the variable cost lines: the wider the angle, the greater the change.

Figure 72 shows a contrasting business, with relatively high variable costs and relatively low fixed costs.

Notice that the break-even point is sooner than in Figure 71, and the margin of safety correspondingly larger. The rate of change of

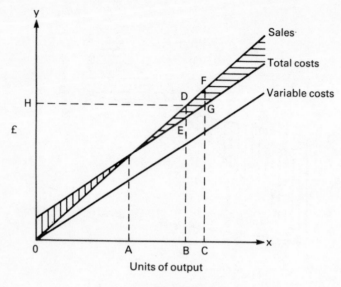

Figure 72

profit is much less: from DE to FG in Figure 72 is much less than in Figure 71 for the same change in activity from 0B to 0C. It is, of course, possible for the starting position to be the same in each case: the same profit, DE, being earned on the same sales income 0H. Therefore the profit margin (profit % sales) would indicate identical performance. But the *potential* performance is very different should market demand change. If the market expands, the business represented in Figure 71 will prosper much more in profit terms than the business in Figure 72; while if the market contracts, it is better to be the type of business illustrated in Figure 72, than the one in Figure 71, from the point of view of minimizing the fall in profit and the possibility of incurring a loss.

Changes to Cost Structure

It is usually possible for managers to change the cost structure of a business. One way is to initiate cost reduction programmes, so lowering the amount of fixed costs in total or the variable costs per unit. For businesses which embody new ventures, the cost structure may also change due to the learning-curve effect, whereby employees waste less resources as they become more skilled in carrying out what were, initially, unfamiliar tasks. More fundamental changes may also be contemplated, e.g. a decision to stop subcontracting and start own manufacture will probably lower the variable costs and raise the fixed costs.

Other Relevant Changes

Changes need not be in cost structure alone: selling prices may be altered, so changing the slope of the sales line, with corresponding effects on break-even point, margin of safety and rate of change of profit. Where more than one product is sold and where the contribution per unit differs between products, then a change in the product mix will also alter the break-even point, the margin of safety and the rate of change of profit.

Activity Measures

In Figures 71 and 72, activity was measured in terms of units of output, but alternative ways of measuring activity might have been adopted. Basically, the choice is between a measure related to output, or one related to input. There is also the choice between measurement in non-money or in money terms. Some alternative measures to units of output are: numbers of units sold, sales value of units sold, standard hours produced (the standard-hours equivalent of the number of units produced), actual hours worked (labour or machine hours), percentage of capacity utilized (capacity often being defined in terms of an hours base). Measures of activity based on hours or value have the advantage of enabling charts to be drawn for multi-product situations, where the various products, normally measured in dissimilar units, e.g. bottles and packs, can be expressed in terms of a common denominator. For example, suppose that a business makes two products: product A in bottles and product B in packs. Product A takes ½ hour to make, while B takes ¾ hour. These are the standard times set for standard costing purposes. An output of 500 As and 1,000 Bs would therefore represent 1,000 standard hours of work (500 × ½ standard hour) + (1,000 × ¾ standard hour).

Factors Affecting the Interpretation of a Break-Even Chart

There are a number of factors to be borne in mind when using break-even charts such as the ones in Figures 71 and 72. Some of these we discussed in Chapter 3: that the split between fixed and variable costs, on which the figures depend, may be approximate; that the variable costs per unit of activity, the amount of fixed costs and the selling price are assumed to remain constant over the range being considered. Where a break-even chart relates to a multi-product situation, there is an added assumption that either the various products are sold at the same contribution per unit of activity, or that the product mix remains constant, over the range being considered.

In Chapter 4 we saw how different profit and loss figures could be obtained by the use of direct-costing and full-costing principles, and that these differences only arose when there was a build-up or run-down of stocks, i.e. when sales and output were out of balance. The break-even chart calculates profit in line with direct-costing principles, so that the profit shown on the chart need not agree with the profit shown in the profit and loss account. It will not do so if the latter has been drawn up on full-costing principles and sales and output are out of balance.

Calculating Break-Even and Profit Variation

Instead of drawing a chart it is possible to calculate break-even arithmetically.

Figure 73 repeats the data first used in Figure 47, showing a

| | PRODUCTS | | | |
	A	B	C	Total
	£'000	£'000	£'000	£'000
Sales	60	110	200	370
Variable costs	18	35	70	123
Contribution	42	75	130	247
Fixed costs				200
Profit				47

Figure 73

business selling three products A, B and C. The total contribution they create is £247,000 which is more than is needed to cover the fixed costs of £200,000. Break-even will therefore occur when total sales creates a total contribution of no more than £200,000.

This level of sales can be found as shown below:

Since £247,000 of contribution is created by £370,000 of sales
£200,000 of contribution is created by $\dfrac{£370,000}{£247,000} \times £200,000$ of sales

$= £300,000$ sales (approx.)

In other words, break-even sales (£) is found by the formula:

$$\text{Sales £} \times \frac{\text{Fixed costs}}{\text{Contribution}}$$

The extent to which profit varies when there is a change in the level of activity can also be calculated arithmetically. For example, Figure 73 shows that:

a contribution of £247,000 is created by sales of £370,000; therefore a contribution of £67 (approx.) is created by sales of £100.

In other words, profit will rise or fall by about £67 for every £100 of sales gained or lost. (Notice the assumption, outlined earlier, of a constant product mix in a multi-product situation.)

Finance Structure

The way in which a business is being financed is another major element of financial structure, which affects one of the profitability ratios in particular: net profit after tax as a percentage of shareholders' capital.

Figure 74 illustrates three different companies, each with the same total amount of capital employed, but with different policies regarding the source from which the capital is being obtained.

Figure 74 shows that each company uses £300 of capital, but that A obtains its capital entirely from shareholders; while B has obtained ⅔ from shareholders and ⅓ from long-term loans; and C has obtained ⅓ from shareholders and ⅔ from long-term loans.

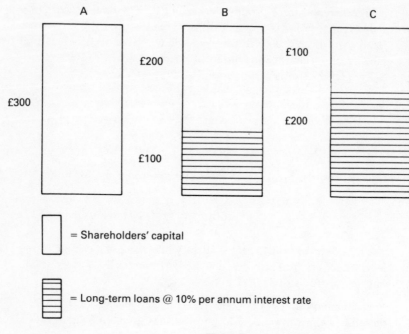

Figure 74

Suppose that profit before deducting interest and tax is £60 in each case. This represents a 20% return for each, measured in terms of the profit before interest and tax as a percentage of shareholders' capital plus long-term liabilities (one of the profitability ratios

	A £	B £	C £
Profit before interest and tax	60	60	60
Interest	—	10	20
Net profit before tax	60	50	40
Tax	30	25	20
Net profit after tax	30	25	20
Shareholders' capital	300	200	100
Net profit after tax % Shareholders' capital	10	12½	20

Figure 75

outlined earlier in the chapter). But the effect of increasing the proportion of loans is to alter the return on shareholders' capital, measured in terms of profit after tax as a percentage of shareholders' capital. This is shown in Figure 75, where, for simplicity, tax is assumed to be 50% of profit.

Figure 75 clearly shows that as the loan proportion increases so the return on shareholders' capital increases. This is because the management of the business are borrowing money at a rate of interest (10%) and investing it at a higher rate (20%). The greater the proportion of capital obtained on those terms, the more the shareholders benefit in terms of the percentage return they obtain on their capital.

Borrowing can, of course, have the opposite effect. This is seen in Figure 76 where £24 of profit before interest and tax is earned by each business, representing an 8% return on the shareholders' capital plus loan capital.

	A £	B £	C £
Profit before interest and tax	24	24	24
Interest	—	10	20
Net profit before tax	24	14	4
Tax	12	7	2
Net profit after tax	12	7	2
Shareholders' capital	300	200	100
Net profit after tax % Shareholders' capital	4	3½	2

Figure 76

Figure 76 shows that to borrow increasing proportions of capital at a rate of interest (10%) greater than the return obtained (8%), is to worsen progressively the return on shareholders' capital. Note also that the range of variation in the return on shareholders' capital increases as proportionately more capital is obtained by means of loans. In company A the shareholders' return oscillates from 10% to 4%, in company B from 12½% to 3½%, in company C from 20% to 2%: all for the same change in profit before interest and tax.

Of course, the different finance structures of the three companies also create different solvency ratios: the ratio of long-term liabilities to capital employed; and interest cover.

Linking Cost and Finance Structure

We saw earlier that cost structure is a major factor affecting the extent to which profit varies when there is a change in the level of activity of a business. For example, when a business has a cost structure as in Figure 71, profit variations are much more than is the case in Figure 72, for the same changes in activity.

We have also just seen that the same changes in profit before interest and tax can have a different effect on the return on shareholders' capital depending upon the finance structure of the business.

Therefore, when assessing the structure of a business and its likely effect upon the shareholders, managers must consider the *combined* effect of the cost structure and the finance structure: the cost structure will determine how profit varies with activity, and the finance structure will determine how the return on shareholders' capital varies with profit.

Changes to Finance Structure

The finance structure of a company may be changed by the company raising or repaying loans; issuing and selling shares, or buying back shares already issued; retaining profits or paying dividends. In all these ways the proportions between shareholders' capital and loans will change.

Working Capital Structure

A number of decisions made by managers affect the current assets and current liabilities of a business, and therefore the liquidity ratios discussed earlier in this chapter. These decisions will also have an effect on whether cash flows into or out of the business, when there is a change in market demand.

Figure 77 shows the cycle for a manufacturing business: raw material is converted into work in progress and then into finished goods, which are sold to customers (debtors), who pay cash, which is used to pay the suppliers (creditors), who send more raw material, and so on. At the stage of converting raw material into work in progress and then into finished goods, cash is also used to pay for the conversion costs.

The decisions which are embodied in this cycle are:

the buying price of the raw material
the conversion costs in processing the raw material
the selling price in selling the finished goods to the customers
the time delays at each stage
– between the receipt of raw material and its issue to production
– between starting the production process and finishing it
– between creating a finished product and selling it
– between sending an invoice to a customer and receiving cash from him
– between receiving an invoice from a supplier and paying cash to him.
– between incurring conversion costs and paying for them.

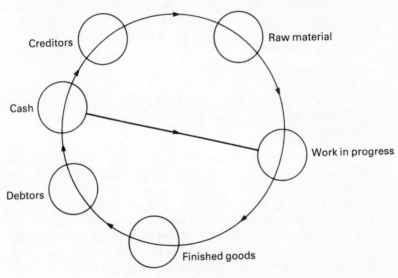

Figure 77

In contrast, Figure 78 shows the cycle for a retailer who sells stock for cash, which is used to pay the suppliers (creditors), who send more stock, and so on.

The decisions which are embodied in this cycle are:

the buying price of the stock

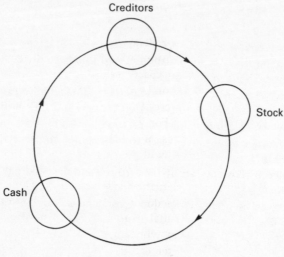

Figure 78

the selling price of the stock
the time delays
– between receiving the stock and selling it
– between receiving an invoice from a supplier and sending cash
to him.

It is clear that these two different cycles are likely to produce different current asset and current liability figures and different liquidity ratios.

Moreover, the cash-flow consequences of growth or decline in market demand are also likely to be different. For example, the business represented in Figure 77 could be an initial cash-loser with growth of market demand, because the cash outflow caused by increased buying of raw materials and increased conversion costs could initially exceed the cash inflow from sales.

In contrast, the business represented in Figure 78 could be an immediate cash-generator with growth of market demand. This will especially be the case if the stock sells quickly and the creditors are made to wait some time before they are paid. In this case, increased market demand could mean that stock is sold for cash and replenished on credit, several times over, before the creditors start to be paid.

Changes to Working Capital Structure

We saw earlier that the current assets and current liabilities of a business are affected by decisions in up to five main areas: buying price (including conversion costs), selling price, stock turnover, debtors' turnover and creditors' turnover. Of course, it may not be possible for managers to exercise more than a limited influence on some of these decisions. For example, selling prices may be determined by market forces, and the terms of trade acceptable to suppliers may not be altered without their agreement. But in many cases it is possible for managers to revise their decisions, or exercise sufficient influence on the situation, so as to create a new working capital structure, with consequent changes in the liquidity ratios and in the cash flow potential from changes in market demand. Some examples of changes which managers could consider are: tighter stock control, tighter credit control; negotiating cheaper purchase prices from suppliers; reducing conversion costs; obtaining advance payments from customers; negotiating with suppliers for them to hold stocks and provide more frequent deliveries; obtaining stock on consignment terms.

Source and Application of Funds Statement

A useful listing of changes taking place in the assets and sources of finance of a business is to be found in a statement known as a source and application of funds statement. This summarizes the changes taking place in the assets and the sources of finance of a business between two consecutive balance sheet dates.

The concept of source and application of funds can best be understood by means of a simple example. Suppose that an individual has a car that he wishes to sell. It will sell for £5,000. When he bought the car he borrowed some money and still owes the lender £1,000, which he has to repay if he sells the car. He intends to buy a new car costing £11,000 and approaches his bank manager for a new loan. The manager will lend no more than £6,500; therefore he has to use £500 of his existing cash.

A source and application of funds statement summarizes these figures, as shown in Figure 79.

	SOURCES OF FUNDS	
	£	£
Sale value of old car	5,000	
New loan	6,500	11,500

	APPLICATIONS OF FUNDS	
	£	£
Cost of new car	11,000	
Repayment of old loan	1,000	12,000
Reduction in cash		500

Figure 79

Figure 79 consists of a list of the changes taking place in the individual's list of assets and sources of finance: selling the old car removes an item from his list of assets, while raising a new loan adds an item to his list of sources of finance; similarly, buying a new car adds an item to his list of assets, while repaying an old loan removes an item from his list of sources of finance.

A list of assets and sources of finance is, of course, found in a balance sheet, so that a source and application of funds statement is essentially a list of changes taking place in the assets and sources of finance of a business between two consecutive balance sheet dates.

Typical entries in a business source and application of funds statement are shown in Figure 80.

Cash Flow Statement

In the UK, a cash flow statement is generally provided for share-holders with the balance sheet and profit and loss acount, to make up a trio of accounts relating to their company. Where consolidated accounts are provided, the trio will generally include a consolidated cash flow statement. An example of a UK cash flow statement is shown in Figure 81 where negative numbers are shown in brackets. Note that Figure 81 contains the same items as Figure 80 but they are listed in a diffferent sequence and with different sub-headings.

Summary

In this chapter we have been looking at four major themes which are relevant in analysing a business, from a financial viewpoint: financial performance, financial condition, financial structure and changes to financial structure. The appraisal of performance focused on profitability ratios, while the appraisal of condition focused on liquidity and solvency ratios. The impact of the finan-cial structure of a business was considered under three headings:

cost structure, finance structure, and working capital structure. Changes to the structure were also considered, and this led to an outline of a source and application of funds statement, as a useful summary of changes taking place in the assets and sources of finance of a business between two consecutive balance sheet dates; and a relisting of these changes to form a cash flow statement.

SOURCE AND APPLICATION OF FUNDS STATEMENT

	£	£
Sources of Funds		
Net profit before interest, tax and depreciation	x	
Sale proceeds of fixed assets sold	x	
Share issue	x	
New loans	x	
Interest received	x	
Reduced stocks	x	
Reduced debtors	x	
Increased creditors	x	x
Applications of funds		
Purchase of fixed assets	x	
Repayment of loans	x	
Increased stocks	x	
Increased debtors	x	
Reduced creditors	x	
Dividends paid	x	
Interest paid	x	
Tax paid	x	x
		x
Increase/reduction in cash		

Figure 80

CASH FLOW STATEMENT

	£	£
Operating activities★		x
Interest received	x	
(Interest paid)	x	
(Dividends paid)	x	
Returns on investments and servicing of finance		x
(Tax paid)	x	
Taxation		x
Sale proceeds of fixed assets sold	x	
(Purchase of fixed assets)	x	
Investing activities		x
Net cash inflow (outflow) before financing		x
Share issue	x	
New loans	x	
(Repayment of loans)	x	
Financing		x
Increase (reduction) in cash		x
	£	
★Net profit before interest, tax and depreciation	x	
Reduced (increased) stocks	x	
Reduced (increased) debtors	x	
Increased (reduced) creditors	x	
Operating Activities	x	

Figure 81

INDEX